BOLD

VISION

A LEADER'S PLAYBOOK FOR MANAGING GROWTH

Sweet Susan –
Live your Vision Always!

PAULA MORAND

MOtivational PRESS
LEADERS IN GLOBAL PUBLISHING

Published by Motivational Press, Inc.
1777 Aurora Road
Melbourne, Florida, 32935
www.MotivationalPress.com

Manufactured in the United States of America.

ISBN: 978-1-62865-457-8

CONTENTS

INTRODUCTION

I F YOU STARTED your own business in the last five years you have lots of company.

More than one million new businesses are launched every year in the United States alone, and another 145,000 in Canada.

In most cases, their owners have great ideas, an impressive skill-set, and a commitment to invest their money and labor into making these new enterprises a success.

Sadly, eight out of ten of them will fail within three years.

These statistics don't even take into consideration new ideas launched from within existing organizations.

As a successful entrepreneur and award-winning mentor rock-star, I believe this is in part due to our total focus on the start-up phase of a business and our lack of attention to the growth phase that must follow.

When entrepreneurs are setting the foundation for their new businesses, there is a wealth of literature and programs to guide them. But once the business is established and they begin to make a reasonable profit, they fall into a status quo pattern.

We forget that the growth phase is even more important than the start-up phase. There is more to gain and more to lose at this second phase.

The question I am most often asked by the entrepreneurs and leaders I mentor is: "The business is up and running well; now, where do I go from here?"

Once your business is operating smoothly and making a profit and your product or service is well received by your customers, it is shocking to consider that if you don't move yourself to the growth phase you may be facing failure within five years.

Even if you are a one-person operation working from your home office, you need to keep an eye open for the green light of growth or you will stumble into the status quo downward slope.

Ultimately, you will be overtaken by growing expenses and competition.

I am writing this book to fill the gap between start-up and the second phase of small business: the growth phase.

In my company, Paula Morand Enterprises, my team and I work with many founders and corporate teams throughout the world to help them push themselves out of their comfort zones and into their growth zone with smart strategy and growth solutions.

In the process, we have developed a highly-effective system to take these talented, clever people from their initial successes into a logical pattern of growth that will keep their business sustainable.

It is not so much a step-by-step process as a gradual, all-encompassing mindset change.

That is the essence of this book.

Whether you sell products from your spare bedroom, write books from your kitchen table, provide life-coaching from your downtown office, motivate people as a professional keynote speaker, do magic acts, or make jewelry, we know you have the makings to take your company to the next level.

All the leaders we work with have one thing in common; they work very hard to make their businesses profitable and within a couple of years after start-up, with diligence and planning, they are pulling in more than $100,000 to $200,000 a year.

If you are encouraged with initial success it is hard to see the downside to what you are doing.

You are successful, but are you sustainable? What can you do to grow to ensure that your business has income from different sources, that it can sustain itself over the long term? How long can you maintain your heavy task load? When can you set aside time to plan and direct your own growth?

I decided to write this book because I believe I can genuinely help you if you have started a successful business and want to move it to the next level.

I will help you achieve the success that you deserve for all your efforts.

I will show you how you can be even more successful and ensure the sustainability of your business to support you and your team for years to come.

As you are mentored on how to grow your business, you will also find yourself taking a personal journey to explore how the same strategies that help your business grow can help you grow.

This is a book that answers the question: "Where do I go from here?"

As the philosopher Seneca said: "If one does not know to which port one is sailing, no wind is favorable."

I cannot find your way for you. But I can give you the knowledge and background to steer you to your own map and the clues to find your own destination.

Join me on this exciting journey that will change your business and change your life.

CHAPTER ONE

DO YOU HAVE A WINNER'S MINDSET?

"Winning is following the instincts that drive the heart and mind."

– Hermann J. Steinherr

WHEN I FIRST LEARNED to drive I was timid about travelling from one place to another even on the quiet streets of my area of the city.

Through unexpected circumstances, one day, I suddenly found myself driving on an eight-lane super highway.

I was totally petrified.

Initially I thought I would just stay in the slow lane on the right. It would be safer there.

But it was not, because vehicles were constantly approaching me from my right to enter the super-highway. I either had to swerve into the adjacent lane which was challenging because I had not planned far enough ahead to do so easily, or slow down and let the incoming cars get ahead of me.

I opted for the latter and kept falling farther behind. It was very late when I reached my destination and I was exhausted. I resolved next time I would at least try to find the courage to make it to one of the faster lanes.

As circumstances would have it, I soon found myself back on a super-highway. I slowly and carefully worked my way to the middle-lane and I had a much better driving experience. But when traffic slowed with trucks ahead of me, I looked longingly at the fast track and wondered if I dared move over there.

When I started my first business, it felt a lot like my initial driving experiences.

I started small, on the slow lane, and I was proud that I was at least behind the wheel and moving forward.

Very quickly I realized if I did not make a move to another track, I would be constantly bombarded by others moving into my field and many of them would get ahead of me.

Eventually, I would end up going slower and slower and I might not even make it to my goal if I didn't find a way to grow and move faster.

I learned that growth is tough and most of us are a little afraid of it. We are the species who sought shelter in caves and preferred to stay there in our safe comfort zone, emerging only when we needed to sustain ourselves.

Today, we build our caves differently. They are our comfortable work places, whether home offices or rented spaces. If we emerge with sufficient revenue to keep food on our family's table and clothes on our backs, we consider we are doing okay.

We might like to have more revenue, but we are a little afraid that if we leave our cave we might not find another. Or we might be eaten by a beast that lurks outside.

I totally sympathize with entrepreneurs who have just gotten their business going and are really concerned about the ramifications of taking the next step.

It is hard to leave a comfort zone. There are days when you may doubt you have the courage to do it.

When I had to leave mine, I worried a great deal about how it would disrupt my life.

But growth done right can be an amazing journey.

I am an entrepreneur and have been for more than 20 years. In that time, I learned when to stay in the middle of the traffic, and when to pull into the fast lane. I learned the slow lane is not a good option.

From acquisitions to failures, and to award-winning success, my emotions have run deep and my passions have been pushed to their limits and my wallet well worn.

I can tell you, honestly today, that when you start to grow your business you come up against both anticipated and unexpected obstacles and neither one is welcome. Because of this, forgive yourself for wanting to stay where you are. It is understandable to not want to add to the chaos and disruption in your life.

But deep down, everyone reading this book has the courage to move from the lane they are in to a faster one, and make it a successful manoeuver.

You really are wired that way, even if you do not realize it yet.

We are all capable of change and growth as an inherited pattern of behavior.

To test that, consider if you can make your brain change something for a few minutes.

What if you know you load the dishwasher efficiently, but your spouse insists another way is better? You oblige while he or she is watching to save a disagreement. But when they are not around and you have to load it again, you revert back to the way you believe to be best.

In this book, I am challenging you to change your mind about a few things and keep it changed, not to revert back when you stop reading my words.

By the time you reach the last chapter, some of the beliefs you hold true right now will be gone forever.

Even if you try to retrieve them the minute you close the book, your new thoughts will crowd in and demand to be considered alongside what you thought you knew.

That means that you will have grown, and simultaneously, you will be ready to grow your business.

I have always favored a holistic approach to growth that is much more than just a series of steps to be followed. If you mentor by just listing steps, just as soon as you walk away the person reverts back to doing what they always did.

But if you grow new attitudes, that can't happen. Your powerful brain won't let you revert.

That is why our first goal to growing your business is to adapt a winning mindset.

You can do it faster and easier than you think, even if right now you don't think you have the capacity to change.

Let us take a minute and look at the human brain and how it develops in terms of absorbing knowledge and beliefs that guide us through life, and how difficult it may be to change some of those beliefs.

The basic things that we learn and believe about life enter our crucial brain circuits when we are about two years old. In fact, half of the way our adult brain is configured stems from what happens to us from birth to two years.

The rest of it, that other 50 percent, fills up as we have life experiences and begin to observe our world. Sometimes what we see conflicts with what we learned when we were two and it puzzles us.

Take the generation born when the world was thought to be flat. Imagine how it would feel to be 50 years old, to stare at the horizon, and to comprehend for the first time that what you totally believed for the first half century of your life was false.

You would not fall off the world if you sailed to the edge of what you could see. Instead, you would just keep on sailing around and around to new continents and cultures and challenges. How difficult would that have been to accept?

Would you go to bed each night still convinced that the new scientists were wrong and that the whole pack of them were going to find out pretty soon when they sailed into a deep, dark hole? Or would you fall asleep with visions of opportunities in new worlds that you could now consider seeing?

Accepting that the world was not flat showed mankind something quite tremendous. It showed us that we are constantly making new brain cells and new neural connections all through our adult lives, and we are capable of lasting change. In fact, our brains are perfectly suited to doing that.

In other words, none of us are really wired to keep doing what we have always done. None of us are really wired to think that what we believed to be true yesterday is necessarily true today. We are all wired to grow in innovation, in creativity, in intelligence, and in the ability to adapt to new knowledge.

This is a great miracle of life. We are actually wired to change, to be innovative, and to see our world in new ways.

Whether you realize it or not, every day your brain is making choices about what you want to hold onto and what you want to release. Each day, you have about 50,000 to 70,000 thoughts. You can change the pattern of what your brain seeks out and saves and prompts you to act on just by changing your thoughts.

That means that as entrepreneurs and leaders, you have to believe that you are capable of taking your business to the next level. Once you adopt that winning mindset you will start to have better and more creative ideas on how to accomplish it.

It takes courage to start to consciously take control of your thoughts and eliminate all the negative self-thoughts and negative inner dialogue that plague us all. You will find strategies to do that along with a lot of other useful information in the coming chapters.

You will learn:

» How to identify growth areas for your business and how to manage that growth.

» How to increase your sales revenue and perfect your sales techniques.

» How to handle follow-up and follow-through processes with clients.

» How to turn your social media connections into confirmed clients.

» How to master the art of innovation.

» How to diversify your product and service offerings.

» How to balance risks and opportunities.

» How to deliver an amazing customer experience.

» How to incorporate a reliable framework for making decisions.

» How to use your time effectively by creating realistic schedules.

» How to incorporate our effective CAR strategy (Consistency, Alignment and Repetition).

» How to build your strategic content plan.

» How to enhance your communications strategies.

Imagine yourself more successful than you are. When your subconscious brain nags you and suggests "Oh, you can't do that," fight back and say "I can do it.

I am smart and resourceful. I have the ability to make this happen."

Gradually, the same brain you inherited from the species that accepted that the world was not flat accepts that you are capable of more success. Your visualization and your thought patterns begin to change and when that happens, people begin to respond differently to you.

When you believe in yourself, others believe in you too.

THE CONQUER ZONE

Start now to visualize your new business. How will it look different from the way it looks now? What will you be doing in your new work day?

How will your business be different now that you have a winning mindset? Will it make you bolder about the things you will seek?

What negative thoughts do you need to release? List five of them.

What positive thoughts will you counter them with? List your new thoughts.

ENERGIZER

"And the day came when the risk to remain tight in a bud was more painful than the risk it took to blossom."

– Anais Nin

CHAPTER TWO

HOW DOES YOUR BUSINESS GROW?

"Let go of certainty. The opposite isn't uncertainty. It's openness, curiosity and a willingness to
embrace paradox, rather than choose up sides.
The ultimate challenge is to accept ourselves
exactly as we are, but never stop trying to learn
and grow."

– Tony Schwartz

WHEN YOUR MINDSET is ready to grow your business you will be asking yourself "how do I get started?"

The obvious and traditional way is to dig out your latest financial report and start crunching numbers.

I have never encouraged obvious thinking.

Originally, that was because I didn't know all the obvious things to do, so I had to figure things out as I went along.

I remember getting my first client, and then my second and my third.

Twenty-three years later, I have tens of thousands of clients in various countries and won a myriad of awards and accolades. This is my 15th book about business and human potential and many books have reached best-seller status.

The point is, I honestly never really saw all that coming when I was basking in the success of getting my first 10 clients. I thought that was as good as it might get.

Along the way, I learned that growth is an inevitable part of entrepreneurship. If you don't keep moving to a faster track, you will begin to slow and fall back as others move ahead.

But if your first business has just reached its stage of profitability, you have an overwhelming urge to just keep doing what you did to get there. After all, you are succeeding while lots of others are failing, so why push yourself to further growth?

As I tracked what I did through my growth as an entrepreneur, I kept asking myself questions like that and eventually I recognized a pattern of six questions that need to be asked and answered to truly accept that growth is necessary.

It is important to consider each of these six questions within the context of your own business.

That is because to really commit to growth you have to believe that you need it.

So here are the six questions to challenge your thinking as a visionary. These are the same questions that I and my growth minded clients ask themselves and a composite of the answers we typically receive.

Question 1: Why can't I simply keep doing what I am doing? It seems to be working.

Answer: If I do not grow my business bigger than myself, ultimately, I will simply run out of energy. All of us have just 24 hours a day, and during that time we need to eat, sleep, sustain important relationships, and conduct all the aspects of life.

During the start-up phase of my business, I put in incredible hours and energy. To keep it successful, I will need to dig still deeper and look for more and more from myself. Without sufficient growth to hire help, I will simply burn myself out.

Already you may find that your days are becoming a never-ending series of tasks and appointments with clients, with no time to get new clients or produce new services or products and grow.

Growth is about finding a way to make more people your clients and more products or services to create new revenue streams. It is also a way to get more people working for you to help you achieve your goals. That allows you time to find new markets and target them effectively.

Question 2: Why will I fall behind if my product or service is really good?

Answer: No matter how good my product or service is, and how reasonable my prices are and how happy my clients are, I am just one smart competitor away from losing some share of my market.

Holding onto my piece of the pie isn't enough. The pie will grow and I will grow and I need to secure my space for the future.

Question 3: But if I keep my current customers, won't that be enough?

When the market grows and I don't I am actually getting smaller, not standing still. My piece of the whole economic pie becomes a little less.

If I am offering a popular service or product and I believe it will get even hotter in the future, I have to be able to capture more of the market.

Right now, if I were to assess myself honestly I don't even have time to stay totally on top of trends in my industry.

Question 4: Why should I work harder if I am currently making enough money for a good life?

Answer: I need to work smarter, not harder.

Would I work for anyone else who didn't increase my pay-check for five years?

Why would I put up with that kind of treatment from myself? My skills are growing every year, and so should my revenue.

Question 5: Can't I weather an economic storm better if I stay small?

All things are uncertain. The stronger I am, the better I will be able to survive a downturn in the economy.

Do I know the potential threats to my business? What steps am I taking to prepare myself to handle them? Am I selling what the market needs...am I solving the right problems for my customers?

Question 6: Why do I still need to offer more products and services?

Answer: The more I diversify and find opportunities to add to my current products and services, the more secure my company will be. Often this is accomplished just by broadening my mindset, not with a lot of extra work.

I can see now how growth may be an option I need to consider.

When I ask other entrepreneurs about the early days of their business, they tell me stories about running in perpetual crisis mode. A fire starts and they put it out. In the distance they can see another spark igniting and so on. The stress is unrelenting. I am currently experiencing that.

Once my business is established, I can't keep operating like that. Time spent trouble-shooting is just putting out a fire; it is not propelling me forward.

QUESTIONS LEAD TO RESOLVE

Now that you have asked yourself these crucial questions and compared yourself with what others have answered, you can see the need for the right systems to be in place, the right information to be at your fingertips, and the right people to help you.

You need to learn how to increase your sales, diversify your products and services, and hike up your revenue, all the while being mindful of your costs.

Every major move you take towards business growth is going to require the same careful planning that accompanied your original business launch.

Consider growing your business as a sort of marathon. It is a rare occasion that anybody running a marathon crosses the finish line without first having committed to running the race.

Commitment is the foundation from which you will set your goals and measure every activity to grow your company.

It is also a crucial component of your personal leadership development that allows you to build a new disciplined approach to living and working with excellence.

I have never worked with a client to help them grow their business without watching them simultaneously grow themselves.

When you commit to the growth of your business, you are making an earnest pledge to achieving greatness, knowing that even when things are difficult that you will stay on track and follow through to the end.

Committing to set priorities makes a world of difference because doing the right actions at the right times aligned with the right focus will always help you to stay true to your goal.

In my last book, *Bold Courage,* I reminded readers about the Star Wars movie, *Return of the Jedi,* and how the character Yoda explains commitment best when he spoke to the young Jedi, Luke Skywalker, during his training.

Yoda said: "Do or do not. There is no try."

The same can be said for your commitment to grow your business. You are either committed or you are not; there is no grey area. You can't be a little bit committed and stay on track. You've got to have drive, be ready to give it all, and above all, believe in your vision.

Once you have considered the crucial questions and answers and made your commitment, you will next have to develop the ten aspects of a winning mindset that will get you through the remainder of the process.

These aspects are:

1. **Know why you want to grow** – Do not grow just for the sake of growth. Growth is only good when you know new ways to add value to your product or service. Growth is only good when you know you can deliver more to your customers and do it well. Growth is only good when it is in sync with the growth in your life.

2. **Know how you want to grow** – Consider what offerings would enhance your business and be fulfilling to you. You have to play to your business's strengths and your own strengths. Growth in your business must be more than just a labor, it has to be a labor of love. You have to identify your ideal market of people most likely to love spending time with you and your product or service and those you want to spend time with as well.

3. **Know how to measure your growth** – How will you measure the success of your growth? What kind of system will you put in place to know if you are moving along the right track?

What are the right things I should be focused on to measure success?

4. **Spot growth opportunities** – When you align your vision and strategy, you will enter a kind of enhanced awareness where it becomes easier to spot opportunities and to grow your relevance to your customers. It also gets easier to weed out the distractions and false notions that are pure opportunism and not authentic growth. As you develop the skill of making decisions determined by their relevance to your goal, it allows for adaptability and flexibility, placing priorities on certain segments and therefore releasing the burden of having to balance everything at once.

5. **Eliminate the clutter** – Once you have made your plan and aligned your priorities, eliminate all the clutter that comes your way. Clutter in this case is anything that is irrelevant to what you are trying to achieve. From today forward, each and every step you take to business growth must be weighed against your desired outcome. One of the major causes of stress and of time lost in business growth is the clutter we allow into our mental process. This clutter primarily takes the form of negative thoughts centered on fear of failure and doubt that you can do it. If you get bogged down in clutter, you are apt to over-

spend, overextend and underperform and wake up at a destination you never planned to go.

6. **Assess opportunities relevant to your goals** – Opportunities are only good if they get you to your intended goal. In my own life, I have sometimes fallen prey to the shiny penny syndrome. Whenever I see a new idea it sparkles in the sunshine and I want to scoop it up. But shiny pennies won't make you rich; well-considered plans and strategies do. When you make commitments and conquer them, you will find that both you and your business are energized. You will be engaged to look for the next challenge to get closer to your goals, and your self-confidence will grow.

7. **Express willingness to look past the obvious** – Sometimes what appears to be too difficult ends up being the most rewarding opportunity. For example, in 2009, I said yes to an opportunity to sit on a global advisory council for women's issues for an international, non-governmental, charitable organization. Most people with my schedule would have said no to the offer right away. But the years have taught me not to make snap decisions, but to instead consider them and recognize if the requested action could align with my business and personal goals. In this instance, it expanded my global vision and allowed

me to branch out greatly as an entrepreneur, speaker and community builder.

8. **Do your research and preparation** – In the example mentioned above, I did a SWOT (Strengths, Weaknesses, Opportunities and Threats) analysis and saw that much of my brand or product is my own willingness to try to make a difference to others in life. This fit. Six months later I joined a team of seven people in Liberia, West Africa, a poor nation still impacted by a horrific 16-year civil war. My work there gave me an amazing new perspective on my business and my ability to speak with more understanding and wisdom about the world and the human condition.

9. **You can't do what you've always done** – Just like you can't grow the same crop in the same soil all the time, or it will start to yield less and deplete the soil, you can't do the same things in the same way all the time or you will start to stagnate in your business. When you step far outside of your comfort zone you often discover, as I did, that you were right where you always wanted to be.

10. **Ask yourself "what else is possible?"** – Being open to amazing possibilities allows you to reframe your ideas about what is possible

and think differently and that is the impetus for authentic growth. When you adopt the winning mindset that you are willing to grow, you need to know what opportunities look like. You are limited only by your ability to consider possibilities to see yourself successful beyond what your current situation is. You have to be willing to see possibilities and your potential for further greatness.

Are you beginning to realize what a winning mindset looks like?

Ask yourself now: "Am I willing to believe that I can play a vital role in the success of my business? Am I willing to make it happen and do I believe I am worthy of great things?"

As you can see, to grow a business you must also grow yourself. You must be willing to see yourself differently than your current circumstances present.

When I was growing up, I was a good swimmer and my father used to challenge me to swim underwater laps. Each time I was successful he would up the ante and make it more challenging for me. I would swim as far as I could until my lungs hurt. Every time he challenged me, I would dive into the pool trusting that my lungs would carry me farther than the last time I attempted it.

That is a good analogy of how you learn to grow your business.

You have developed strength and resourcefulness and you know how to operate your business.

But now you have to test how long you can hold your breath under the water. You have to trust that what you know and what you have done already will be strong enough to take you farther.

THE CONQUER ZONE

When is the best time to grow your business? It is now.

Without even realizing it, many entrepreneurs live in a reactive state ready to solve the next big problem instead of planning and envisioning new product and service opportunities to grow their business.

In this exercise, I want to challenge your thinking about what failure could mean to you.

Is it your business that can't make a mistake, or is it you who can't?

Do you need validation every day with your success that your decisions are sound?

Today, give yourself permission to see the value of all your experiences as places of learning and growth. They have value, just as dollars and cents have value.

I know there are numerous books that talk about failure being a great thing, but the actual process of failing doesn't feel good to anyone when they are moving though it.

When you start to grow your business, your success or failure lies in how you learn to deal with your experiences and grow from them. Yes, you will have some mistakes and setbacks, but things will still turn out fine.

Make recognizing what is amazing about you a priority.

Start right now by writing down five things about yourself that are amazing. Keep that list handy so that when you have a tough day, you know that nobody can take those things away from you.

ENERGIZER

If it really was a no-brainer to make it on your own in business, there'd be millions of no-brained, hair-brained and otherwise dubiously brained individuals quitting their day jobs and hanging out their own shingles. Nobody would be left to round out the workforce and execute the business plan.

– Bill Rancie

CHAPTER THREE

HOW TO GET IN
THE BUSINESS GROWTH TRACK

"Business opportunities are like buses; there's always another one coming."

– Richard Branson

TO DRIVE ON THE super-highway you need a steady and reliable vehicle that you can count on to support you regardless of what lane you are in.

When it comes to business growth, that vehicle is your customers.

So, hand-in-hand with asking yourself "How can I grow my business?" you need to be asking "How can I give more value and delight to my customers?"

Growth, for the sake of growth, will miss the mark without a deep understanding of what kind of growth is needed.

Would your customers appreciate more timely delivery of your services? You might need to consider growth from the point of view of getting help to complete projects faster.

Would they like it if you could give them additional services? What are the additional services they request most often that you are not currently providing? What service can you think of that they haven't even considered, but that would delight them?

What part of your product or service do they love, and what additional project would combine with it to make it better?

For example, think about the perfect combination when Johnson & Johnson added Polysporin antibiotics to their Band-Aid strips. Some products just naturally complement each other.

If you sell professional services in your business, why are people buying these specific services? Is it to save time so they don't have to do it themselves? Is it to gain expertise because they don't have the knowledge to do it themselves? Is it to make their lives easier or more fun? Or is it because you help them to make their lives better?

Whatever your answer is, it taps into a well of opportunity. What else could you do to save their time? What additional knowledge could you offer them? What would make your service add even more fun or ease to their lives? How could you make their lives better?

Of all the ways you can grow your company, being able to add value to the lives of your customers is the most authentic and longest-lasting approach. It is also the perspective that will give you more success than any other reason for growth.

Think about some of the biggest, most impressive companies in the world today that proudly insist delighting their customers is their first and foremost motivation.

Disney is unsurpassed in this area, constantly adding new attractions like their Star Wars adventure. Disney's philosophy is that every time a customer interacts with one staff member, it is a moment of truth that measures how well they are doing their job to delight their customers.

So, whether you are asking for directions to the "It's a Small World" ride, wondering when the parade will start, or ordering food, they know you need to have the same pleasant and helpful response.

Another company that has proven delighting customers is the basis for growth is the 105-year-old L. L. Bean in Maine. They deliver outstanding service 365 days a year, a daunting challenge, but they are unwavering in their commitment to accomplish this.

Google is another success story because in every growth phase they focus first on the user, not their own goal or bottom line. They will not let you buy a top placement on a page; they mark advertisements clearly. They understand trust is their most important value.

Amazon knew that it wasn't just enough for their customers to get goods delivered right to their door. They established 24/7 support services because they understood that the ultimate delight for the home shopper comes from being able to shop anytime of the day or night.

Once you know what else you could do to delight your customers the next thing to focus on is sales.

Before you invest hours into developing all the details of the new service or product you think would be crucial to growing your business, you need to figure out if it will sell.

How can you do that?

Advance sales of people wanting your product send a clear signal that you are on the right track. Authors like James Paterson and Janet Evanovich know that the public wants to read more of the adventures of Alex Cross and Stephanie Plum. Amazon only has to send out reminders of the book's arrival months in advance, and people lock in their purchase to be delivered on publication day.

How do you gain sales for your new product or service as you grow your company?

You reach first for the low-hanging and sweetest fruit, and that is your current customers. Test the waters with them first.

Then move to the next layer, which is people who are in contact with your current customers.

Start today by making a list of all the people you know. You may think that it will take forever, but it won't. For most firms, it is a very doable project.

List every single person who is currently a customer. Next list people who once did business with you but who are no longer active customers.

Now make a list of colleagues you worked with along the many roads you took in your careers before you became entrepreneurs.

Next, write down the names of your friends and the people you've meant that you thought were impressive.

Before you know it, you are going to end up with a very large list.

What you have created is a list of people you are in some way connected to.

Now, edit that list with a red pen.

Take out all the people who talk a lot but don't really do anything. Then take away the people who are passive, and the people who don't follow through, and then the people who are very negative and closed to new opportunities. They may end up being your customers someday, but they aren't what you need right now.

Now take a green pen and circle the names of the people who are connectors, who give of themselves and receive new ideas openly. You need people who are open and generous by nature, because they are the people who really connect to other people and are not going through life just for themselves. They are the potential customers and the ones who can help you the most.

Your new list will be a lot smaller than the one you started with, but it will also be a lot more valuable.

Tomorrow, email just four people from that list. Tell them what you want to do and offer them an idea of how you can work together.

If you offer life coaching, for example, and they are credit counsellors, see if you might sometimes work together if one of the issues your client is struggling with is debt. Or, if you are a small business coach, team up with a bookkeeping firm who could help your clients establish good accounts practices. Look for all of these mutually beneficial relationships.

You will find that most of the people on your small list have the potential in some way to work with you and help your business grow. But start small, with just four, and explore this idea to see where it goes.

When you grow this way, your growth will be purposeful. You pick a select target and try to connect solidly with that person, rather than firing off your energy in all directions and ending up with a lot of empty shells but no hits.

Ask to have coffee with your list of connections, a virtual meeting or to go to their offices for a 15-minute meeting just to explore ways you could work together. You don't want to waste each other's time, so you need to arrive at these meetings with some idea of what you want and a very customized pitch to get it. Be focused and clear as to why you want to meet.

Then you need to follow up to make sure that your efforts are not forgotten.

Ford Motor Company grew substantially using this method. Right now they seek out potential new partners by offering access to their 300,000 employees and retirees. In return, they offer discounted sales programs to their partners' employees and retirees. It has been a remarkably effective sales strategy.

Both sets of employees and retirees in the process are delighted to get discounts in excess of the average customer. They feel special because they are getting special considerations.

You may also want to look at franchising your business if you have developed a business model that is successful for you and you can see it working well in other areas.

Franchising allows you to secure additional revenue with the franchise sale and take a franchise fee from the buyer's ongoing revenue, and to have some input on staff training, location, and the look and product authenticity.

Be sure to get a good franchise attorney to help you prepare the legal framework to franchise your business.

In the same vein, you can look at licensing your product, including your corporate name or system. For example, I use Paula Morand Enterprises to protect my various teaching programs, publications, and success programs.

It benefits me two ways: it protects the integrity of my product offering and if others want to use it (such as my Success Tracking System for example), I can collect upfront money or royalties.

For magic acts, songs and stories, software, and product delivery systems, licensing can be a good growth move.

Another growth method is to seek an alliance with a business that fits naturally with yours. For example, a life coach could link up with a personal trainer or a nutrition consultant. An entertainer could link up with the seller of a certain sound system or brand of musical instrument. An accountant could team up with a Cloud based software provider. A health provider could team up with a teaching facility.

You can also grow by targeting new markets.

Suppose that you run a consulting business in which

you help people with their finances and tax issues. The bulk of your clients are middle-aged working people, many of them entrepreneurs.

Targeting a new market could mean recognizing how many newly-retired people in your community are starting their own businesses. You tap into that growth market. Specialize some services for the over 55 age group. Their basic needs are the same as your other clients, but by packaging your marketing material differently you can appeal directly to them.

Become the specialist in your area in helping people launch their dream business after their first career is completed.

The important thing when you are planning to grow by targeting new markets is to figure out where your new kind of client hangs out and then go there.

As an example of that, think about how Shopper's Drug Mart chain in Canada targets a special Senior's Day every week in an effort to tap into a growing base of senior clients.

Other ways to grow include securing substantial new contracts that will recur on a yearly or seasonal basis. Federal, provincial and municipal contracts are good examples of these marketplaces.

Governments are major buyers of goods and services, and every one of them has an established process for bidding and getting contracts. Most offer regular sessions for new proprietors who want to learn how to bid and prepare specialized proposals. Watch for announcements in your area and follow through to learn the process.

Another growth strategy involves purchasing another business. The big thing when you buy another company is to ensure that there is a reasonable expectation that the customers will follow you. It makes no sense to buy a company if you don't meet first with a sizeable number of their customers and find out if they will do business with you. This is a delicate exercise unless the firm is on the auction block.

You will also need their best and brightest people. Can your rehire the best of the best?

Another thing to consider is whether or not their technology melds with your technology, or if you are facing additional hefty investments in new systems. Expensive integration of technology costs can be hidden and really hinder your takeover, if you are not careful.

For many solopreneurs, a great source of business growth is diversification of their service or product. For example, the trained bookkeeper adds tax preparation to the list of services provided. Once that is going well, they add audit support to their list of services. With the help of an additional person or two during tax season (and this is something semi-retired professionals are sometimes interested in) you can double your yearly income.

Diversification of product and service offerings is a growth strategy that has been effective for me. For example, as a motivational speaker, I diversified to start writing books, motivational products and online programs so I could sell them at the end of my speaking engagements or ensure that people who wanted to learn more could purchase them on-line.

My key messages could also be packed into business courses and one-on-one consulting experiences. This opened up my passion even more for helping visionaries and subject matter experts build smarter business objectives and strategic brand building tactics.

Once you are known as an authority in your field, diversification is an excellent option for your business growth. The good thing about it is that you don't have to keep reinventing the wheel. You develop a good basic product or service and then you sell it in a number of different ways, over and over. Of course, to make it work, you have to be constantly coming up with new messages and new sales programs along with better ways to communicate that speaks to your market.

Diversification allows you to build up multiple streams of income which increases sales and profits.

Every single business, even if it is a one-person show, has the power to diversify and that is a priority method of growth to consider.

THE CONQUER ZONE

Which of the growth strategies presented in this chapter has potential for your business?

Select at least three possible options and write three reasons why each of these could work for you.

Now go back and study the three options. Which has the most potential to truly delight your customers more?

ENERGIZER

"Growth is never by mere chance; it is the result of forces working together."

– James Cash Penney, founder of JC Penney retail chain

CHAPTER FOUR

TOP TECHNIQUES TO GROW YOUR SALES REVENUE

"Nobody talks of entrepreneurship as survival, but that's exactly what it is and what nurtures creative thinking."

– Dame Anita Roddick

SUPER-SALESPEOPLE aren't super because of their supreme confidence, charm, or charisma.

They are extraordinary because they listen and understand their customer's business so well that they can figure out their problems and how the services or products they are selling can solve those problems.

To be adept at that, they are also extraordinary with their knowledge of the products and services they are selling and how they can be adapted to almost any circumstances.

Of all the skill entrepreneurs have difficulty with, I find it is the skill of conducting and closing a sale.

It is almost impossible to recount how many times my team and I meet with creative, amazing clients and see the services or products they have developed.

And then, these talented people turn to us and say "the hard part for me is selling this because, you know, I don't have a sales personality."

It is really time to put the myth of the "sales personality" to rest if you want to get on the growth track.

Every personality is capable of making great sales. It's true!

That is vital to know because, in business, nothing really happens until there are sales.

Sales is nothing more or less than the art of connecting with people, bringing them on board with an idea, negotiating terms for the exchange of that idea, and then closing that deal with the exchange of money.

You will notice that I use the word "idea" as opposed to goods or services. That is because what people are really buying every time is your idea. They believe that what you offer will in some way add value to them in their lives.

Because of their belief in your idea, they give you cash for the manifestation of it, whether it comes in the form of a can of beans, a software program, or a cleaning service.

The good news is that it is much easier to make your idea palatable to your customer today because you can gather a lot of information about them and their needs even before you meet them.

Thanks to the digital age we live in, we can run names of companies and individuals through Google and find out what they do, what services they are expert in, what products they make and/or sell, and things about their location and customer base. A study of their Facebook page will give you keen insight into what is on the minds of their customers as well.

Once you can gather all the data about your customer and their needs you are ready to determine how best to approach them. Remember that you will still be gathering more information about them when you meet them on-line or in person, but your initial research is a good start.

Let's talk first about what you need to know about your customer's business. Remember, as you conduct your research, to boil down the market-speak terms to plain English that you can grasp quickly.

I'm going to use an imaginary company to take you through how this works.

The company is called "Lifespring." On its website we learn it desires to "support your essential life requirements" and that it "empowers you to maximize your endurance and achieve your personal best."

None of that answers the question you need to answer about your customer which is:

"What do they do?"

What they actually do can be summed up very simply after you wade through the branding copy; They sell bottled, carbonated, water that is flavored with natural essential oils.

Your next question about your customer is "Who buys what they create?"

In this case, you see that they sell to spas, sporting events, gyms, and specialty cafés.

Next question is "where are their customers located?" Their customers are all facilities within a 20 mile radius of their bottling plant.

Now, you have a very crucial question to understand your target customer and that is "Why do they sell this product? Did they see it as a gimmick they could make some quick money on? Did they inherit an essential oils plant and decide to branch out? Do they believe that their product has value to quench the thirst of the nation?"

You learn that the founder of the company invented it as a way of giving up drinking too much caffeinated pop. They served their new home-made drinks to others who loved it, and decided to set up a business bottling and selling it.

Is that enough to know? Absolutely not.

Can you find out if their sales are increasing or declining? What is the industry gossip about them? You look to see if there are any industry reports or if they are a publicly traded company. All information can offer clues to problems your customers might be currently undergoing.

Finally, you look to see if there are any special trends in their industry. You discover that in the community where they operate, there is a big discussion going on at city council about adding fluoride to the water. Will this create problems or opportunities for them? That could be one of the areas to bring up in conversation.

What else do you try to determine before you meet a potential client?

Is the person you are meeting with the person who can make the decision to buy? Do all purchases have to be approved by a head office somewhere?

Finally, you need to know how your product can be of value to them.

If you can't answer that last question, in particular, it's going to be tough for you to convince them to buy it if you can't figure out any reason why they should.

So, those are some of the ways you determine information about your potential clients. Doing your research is the foundation of creating your sales strategy.

With this research, you are also better able to gauge if this is a customer that would make sense for you to court. How much could this customer be worth to you? You need to know that, because it helps you figure out how much time and effort you should put into selling to them.

It makes sense to focus the bulk of your efforts on customers who will most likely enhance your revenue the most.

That doesn't mean they have to be huge customers. Keep an eye out for growing companies with great potential to buy more in the future as well. Finally, keep your eye on people in your customer base who are real go-getters, who are likely to keep moving up the ladder with other companies in the future and who, once they build a relationship with you, may want to take you with them.

Remember, that every client needs an electronic file because you need to be constantly updating your intelligence on them. That includes noting their birthdays when their Facebook notification comes up, their holiday trip that the family enjoyed, and trends and developments in their industry.

Add to that any information that is published about their competitors; as soon as major competitors do something, it immediately creates a need for your client to match it or outdo it in some way. Look for any indication of changing buying patterns.

You can already see that nurturing and keeping a client even after you secure them the first time is going to be an ongoing process. It is something you have to keep track of for a portion of each of your busy work days or something you entrust to your sales representative.

This deep personal and professional knowledge about your customer is crucial, but so is a deep knowledge of your own product or service and a keen understanding of what is called in the sales business, your unique selling proposition or USP.

Your unique selling proposition is the reason why people need to buy from you and not your competitors. It could be superiority of your product, versatility of your service, superior value, guarantee, or warranty of your service.

Of course, it could also be that you offer the lowest price for your product of service, but if that is the case, be very careful. It is very, very risky to compete with price alone.

Once you know about your customers, your product or service, all the ins and outs of it, and what makes you distinguished from your competitors, you need to decide which means you will use to sell.

We've been talking a lot about one-on-one meetings since that is traditionally still how many of the biggest sales deals are made. But, it is by no means the only way and, in fact, it may not work for you at all.

In most cases, you should have two or three means at least as avenues to generate sales to your customers.

The face-to-face approach is known as direct sales and it takes a variety of forms that includes direct mail, tele-sales, and e-commerce. That means that you target one specific customer at a time, and make your approach to try to sell to them.

If you are a consultant selling high-end services that are relatively complex, for example, the direct selling of face-to-face meetings may be a primary means of generating revenue.

But, if you are selling jewelry, on the other hand, you may find direct mail or on-line sales campaigns are more cost-effective to create the volume of sales you need. If you are selling one clear-cut service, such as house-painting or driveway paving, you may find tele-sales work best or even tucking a brochure into the door of the neighborhood you are targeting.

Sometimes you will want a retailer or a wholesaler to sell your products. This is referred to as an intermediary to handle your sales. In that case, instead of focusing on many customers, you just focus on servicing and selling to the intermediary.

Whatever sales route you select, always remember that it will be cheaper every time to sell to existing customers than to court new customers. Having said that, if you want to grow your business most effectively you will need to do both.

When you take all of these steps, you are almost ready to build your sales strategy. The missing piece of the puzzle is that you need to know exactly how much you need to sell to meet your revenue targets for each quarter of your year.

That means stopping and getting out your calculator and figuring out how much you need to sell each month of the entire year ahead.

And here is where you can get into trouble as you try to get your company on the fast-track to growth.

Try not to be overly-optimistic. If you are planning to launch a new product or service you cannot plan that it will sell fast right from the start. Project a reasonable, even growth pattern for sales, since new products and services are a bit like household renovations. They inevitably cost more to get on the market than anticipated, they inevitably take longer to get on the market than anticipated, and when they do hit the market, they inevitably take longer to find a buyer than expected.

Once you have built your sales calendar of expectations, monitor it closely to see how accurate your predictions are. It is important to do this because you will get much better with time. You need to see if you are overly optimistic or in some cases, overly-cautious, both of which can cause you problems.

Finally, in creating your sales strategy, you need to do something that we rarely advise. You need to schedule some time out for negative thinking.

In that session, you need to take your product or service and think of all the reasons why someone would not want to purchase it. Write down the objections they might say about it. Is it too expensive? Can they do it without you? Is it necessary when they are not having a good year? Is it necessary if they are having a good year?

Write down each objection and then, when you are done, write down answers to overcome those objections.

Too many times we paint our businesses with rose-colored brushes, because we love what we are doing and we believe in our hearts that others will see the value in what we do if we are just sincere and genuine and enthusiastic enough.

That works in many, many things that you do in life, but sadly, it does not work in sales.

In sales, you have to be harsh with yourself, to consider the downside of your product and take the time to determine really good arguments to overcome these objections. Then you need to couch them in language that is gentle and persuasive.

It's not like you can sit in front of a customer and say "you are wrong about that." But you can say, "I understand what you are saying and I'm glad you raised that point. Another way to look at it is...." Then you present your well-considered alternate argument.

Once the conversation is beginning to repeat itself the experienced sales person needs to gently lead it back on track to handle the closing of the sale.

At this point, you have established that the potential buyer has a problem and the product or service offered can help it.

Never leave a sales meeting with a vague promise of "I'll leave this with you then," or "I'll get back to you soon."

Instead, say "I'll leave this paperwork with you and I'll call back next Tuesday morning if that is okay with you."

Better yet, pull out your smart phone and say, "I'll be back in this area next Monday. Can I drop in at 9 a.m. for a brief follow-up?"

Set a plan, any plan, as long as it is a concrete action and your potential customer agrees to it.

If you have secured your meeting, had a good session and now you want to pull your targeted client out of the funnel and into the contract phase of the sales process, it is time to close the deal.

If you have made a great case for your product and the customer can clearly see its benefit, but nothing is happening, one closure technique is to create a sense of urgency.

One way to do that is to link quick action with the best interests of the client's needs and deadlines.

For example, you could say:

"I know you are interested in using money from this fiscal year's budget to purchase this, but you aren't quite ready for us to start. What if we signed a contract now for services to be delivered next year, but we added a stipulation that the consultation process wouldn't begin until January 10th?"

Or you could say something like:

"I recognize that you need to get this up and running as soon as possible. If I could get this order signed and into the system now, I could pretty much guarantee the work would be completed before the start of the holiday season. We would be far more likely not to have to work around holiday schedules and stuff like that."

When you are using the urgency card to close, make sure that it appears you are thinking of the customer's needs, not your needs. Just because one more sale would help you make your quota this year is no reason to pressure your client.

Never lie and say that the product is only available for a limited time. Nobody ever buys a second product from a liar.

Part of the skill of closure is also knowing when to stop selling and start signing the final deal. An example of that is when you are selling furniture, if the customers start to talk about where they will put the sofa it is time to start talking about how soon you could sign the deal and get it delivered to them.

When you see your customer is convinced and is making signals to wrap it up, go with it. Many a sale has been lost by saying too much.

If you are down to just one objection...usually around how soon you can start or how soon you can finish, introduce the idea of closing the sale now with a condition attached.

Suggest something like: "If I could guarantee a start date a month earlier to meet your schedule, could we write this order up today?"

If the customer pauses for a long time, don't rush to fill the silence with more talk about your product. Wait patiently and let the customer think, no matter how uncomfortable it makes you feel.

Your silence encourages your customer to realize that a decision is needed and helps them to focus on coming up with an answer.

The final part of closing a sale is to ensure that you get the details right. Write up the order and go over its components as you understand them with the buyer.

When the client nods agreement get them to sign the

contract. Always travel with sufficient copies of your contract.

THE CONQUER ZONE

Select a new potential client. In the next 15 minutes, see how many facts you can gather about them. How could your service or product add value to their lives or solve problems for them?

Get your mind into a strategy of how you could best sell to this client.

Set up a meeting and see how well you do.

Practice is the key to refining your sales skills!

ENERGIZER

When you fail to make a sale it is hard on your ego.

Use this quotation to meditate back to a positive place.

> "We need to accept that we won't always make the right decisions, that we'll screw up royally sometimes –understanding that failure is not the opposite of success, it's part of success."
>
> **– Arianna Huffington**

CHAPTER FIVE

HOW TO TURN YOUR CONNECTIONS INTO CLIENTS

"Information flow is what the Internet is about. Information sharing is power. If you don't share your ideas, smart people can't do anything about them, and you'll remain anonymous and powerless."

– Vint Cerf

FIFTEEN YEARS AGO, Bill Gates said there will only be two kinds of businesses in the future: those with an Internet presence and those with no business at all.

All these years later, we know he was right.

But, we also know that just being present on the Internet and garnering thousands of "likes" and "contacts" still doesn't grow your business.

Unless you can find a way to translate those connections with potential customers into actual sales, you will still not be using social media effectively.

Social media remains one of the most cost-effective ways a small business can grow, but you need to have systems of measurement to bring people closer to you, to build strong relationships and trust, and to turn that trust into sales.

When I provide consulting for entrepreneurs and leaders I hear so many people say they would like to pay more attention to their social media presence but they consider it a waste of time. I have also been told that many feel they spend too much time on social media with little to no results.

I answer by asking if they had a brick and mortar shop, would they consider someone coming into their shop a waste of time?

"Of course not," they answer. "Once a customer is in my shop I have a much better chance of selling them something."

The same goes for your social media connections. Once they get in touch with you, even if it is only to download a White Paper or e-book from your website, or subscribe to your newsletter, you have a much better chance of ultimately turning them into a paying customer.

Every person who interacts with you via social media is a potential customer moving into your sales funnel. By building a relationship with you, however shallow or distant it appears in the beginning, they are moving closer to doing business with you.

Researchers at Stanford University did a study five years ago that showed the average person intensely dislikes talking to total strangers. The study, headed by Dr. Simon Gamble, showed that nobody really wants to talk to a stranger. It makes them a little uncomfortable.

They don't want to appear impolite, so they respond, but they are tentative because they have nothing in common with the stranger and don't really know what to say.

But now, with a passing comment on the Internet, you can breeze right past that natural barrier to engaging in conversation and engage your connections.

If they say they like your blog, for example, you can get right back and thank them and tell them that you are researching a whole book on the subject (if that is true) and would they like an email when it is available?

If they say they appreciated your opinion about a subject you can thank them and tell them it came from your experience as a specialist in your field and let them know you are there if they need any help.

You can build credibility and share things about yourself to build up a relationship. You are starting the process of turning a connection into a customer.

You can invite people to willingly part with their emails so you can send them content that adds value to their lives. You can even offer free webinars or courses or even a free consultation.

In essence, social media connections allow you to make cold-calling a thing of the past.

When people do download your material, be sure to follow-up with them over the next few weeks with another document they might enjoy. That is how you continue your courtship.

Make sure that every bit of good content you create is put to good use. For example, if you did a great PowerPoint for your presentation, why not share it on your website and also on SlideShare (http://www.slideshare.net/).

If you made a great video based on your expertise in a subject, why not post it on YouTube? (www.YouTube.com). After Google, YouTube is the world's second largest search engine so take advantage of it. It is a wonderful way to draw your connections closer to you and turn them into customers.

YouTube is a particularly good site if you are offering a professional service or any kind of a performing act. It is where just about everybody goes to get tutorials on every subject imaginable, from fixing a faulty lawnmower to getting health advice or business advice.

Build on your reputation as an expert in your field by getting on there. Explore the kind of material that is already there and see if you can add something unique to the mix.

If all of this sounds like a lot of work, it is. Growing your business using the Internet takes research and time and innovation, but it is a great method of broadening and deepening your customer base.

Adding content to the Internet and gaining potential customers' interest isn't the only way to grow your business on line.

Another excellent way, that I have found really helpful, is to join professional group discussions and enhance relationships that way.

For entrepreneurs looking for new pools of customers, nothing beats LinkedIn. No site offers more groups crying out for connections either.

Keep in mind that it is always easier to sell to someone who knows you even a little, than someone who doesn't know you at all. So use LinkedIn groups to find people who have connections to you.

For example, you might want to link up with people you knew in school and university. Join the Alumni group. Want to follow-up with people who sparked a connection with you at a conference? Join the Conference group, which is generally limited to people who attended a specific conference or who routinely go to the same trade shows or conferences.

Be bold and jump right into the networking group, exchanging professional contact information and doing everything on line to get closer to your connections that you would normally do at a person-to-person networking event.

Professional group associations are useful if you are looking at forming alliances as a way to grow your business.

You can join up to 50 groups. The average person is in about nine groups and that is about the limit most people can handle and keep up with if they are also running a business.

If you are not sure which groups will yield the best clients for your business, go to a LinkedIn page and click on "groups" from the dropdown menu. Type in a word relevant to the topic you are interested in and you will be presented with options.

Don't just join groups that interest you in your business. Join groups where your targeted customers will hang out. Get to know their concerns and how your business might be able to make their lives easier.

The most important thing to remember once you learn the art of making valuable connections on the Internet is to keep the relationships going. So many people exchange one or two comments and then fall into a communications gap from which they never resume a conversation.

When you sense a strong possibility of turning a connection into a customer, keep the exchange of information going. Grow the conversation into the realm where it touches on how you could make their lives easier with your services or products.

Growing your business on the Internet means that you have to be knowledgeable about your field and willing to contribute something of value in exchange for your connection's interest. Ask people their opinions about things and show respect for them. Have conversations about ideas.

Create your LinkedIn strategy using the free options. If it really works well for you, upgrade to one of the Premium levels such as Basic Business that runs about $25 a month.

In all your social media encounters to grow your business find ways to stay in touch with people. If they express interest in your field of business, for example, offer them a free copy of your monthly email. Keep track of their new projects so you can see where your services might be useful to them.

Growing a client base through on-line connections is no different than face-to-face networking. People have to like you and respect you to continue the conversation with you. If you want them to buy from you they have to perceive that what you offer has value and that it will enhance their lives.

The bottom line is that if you have never been contacted for work from your website and if nobody has ever bought anything you sell from your website or social media sites, then it is not really working.

THE CONQUER ZONE

Take some time to do a thorough inventory of your presence on the Internet and create your own report card. Write down what you think is good and what you feel needs more attention. Consider how well you are promoting your business with your on-line customers.

Score yourself from one to ten in the following areas regarding your presence on Facebook, LinkedIn, Instagram, Twitter, and your corporate website.

1. How well are you portraying your company or yourself on line as expert in its field, reliable in its offering, and available when and where people need its services?

2. How high a value are you placing on the customers who already communicate with you on your Internet locations and how are you keeping them as close as good friends? Are you communicating with them regularly and surprising them with your thoughtfulness?

3. Are you finding, targeting and building relationships with people who are most likely to be interested in the product or service you are offering?

4. Are your turning your connections into paying customers?

5. Are you nurturing, tending, and growing your Internet presence by giving it constant attention, good content and frequent expansion into new areas?

Check the visibility of your website using the SEOmoz Trifecta Tool (http://www.seomoz.org/trifecta). Put in your website URL and see what comes up.

What have you got on your website that could work a little harder for you? Have you got a good video that you could also post on YouTube? Have you got a good blog that you should also be posting on LinkedIn and linking to on Twitter?

Finally, make sure that your website is mobile friendly. If it is full of sidebars and design options that don't translate well to a smart phone, that is a mistake. More and more customers are accessing your website from their phones, so be sure that you adapt all your Internet presence to accommodate that.

ENERGIZER

"The Internet is becoming the town square for the global village of tomorrow."

– Bill Gates

CHAPTER SIX

HOW TO MASTER THE ART OF INNOVATION

"Without change there is no innovation, creativity or incentive to improvement. Those who initiate change will have a better opportunity to manage the change that is inevitable."

– William Pollard

WHEN WE THINK about innovation most of us focus on those rare entrepreneurs who one day have that bolt-of-lightning idea strike them.

Against all odds, they run with that idea, overcoming resistance, figuring out the method to make it work, and in the process, make millions.

Ultimately, they earn their place in the business literature of each generation as the superstars.

When people write about innovation they can't resist quoting Thomas Edison saying: "Genius is 1 percent inspiration, 99 percent perspiration."

Dare I say I think that Edison was wrong?

Genius to me is more 50 percent ideas and inspiration, and 50 percent smart work (perspiration). We live in a more complex digital age where there are so many options and so many sources of information that coming up with the business idea that really clicks with people is more difficult than in the simple times in which Edison worked.

The truth is, almost everyone has a brilliant idea, or even several of them, every day of the week.

The challenge of developing an innovative mindset to grow your business is being able to take that idea down the long dark and winding road to implementation and impact.

In other words, you have to have great ideas, but you also need the characteristics and abilities to take that idea and cultivate it and grow it into a reality.

To do that, you need to think differently from the average person, and you need to act differently.

That is what this chapter is about.

Remember that an innovative mindset is like all the mindsets we have been talking about so far; it is evidence of belief in yourself and your abilities to make things happen. It means that you know in your heart you are capable of taking your best ideas and growing them into a new service or product that will delight your customers and add value to their lives.

An innovative mindset is a vital part of the winning growth mindsets and it is the one most centered on the importance of creating value in this world.

It is about finding solutions for those goods and services people want and need, and offering new value and new delight by delivering goods and services that consumers didn't even know they wanted, but which enhance their life greatly.

As a successful entrepreneur wanting to take your business to the next level on the fast track, you need an innovative mindset to create the success you want.

It's what people who have no real concept of how businesses grow, call luck.

When you cultivate an innovative mindset you are able to do four specific things:

» You can create your own luck by noticing good ideas and acting on opportunities.

» You can make luck a regular visitor to your premises through your own perseverance.

» You can make great decisions that are well informed by facts, but also by your keenly developed intuition.

» You can resist the occasional urge to drown in the negative by finding or generating the sunny side of every situation.

Clients often ask me: Aren't creativity and innovation the same thing?

Not exactly.

A good way to distinguish the two characteristics was contained in an article written by Peter Fisk author of *Creative Genius,* which focused on the eight innovative mindsets of Leonardo da Vinci.

Fisk says that creativity is about "divergent thinking." By that he means we are open up to exploring new perspectives, making new connections, and generating more ideas.

Innovation, on the other hand, is about "convergent thinking." That means we have the capacity to evaluate the best ideas, to focus on making them practical and profitable, and then make them happen effectively.

People with an innovative mindset in business are often referred to as "disruptive entrepreneurs." These are the business people who never say "no" before they say "maybe." They don't close doors to opportunity lightly. They listen and they end the conversation with "let me think about it." They are not dismissive, regardless of the source of the idea.

They have what Albert Einstein labeled a "holy curiosity" to learn about things and a well-established trial and error process to assess what they hear. They always, always leave room for outside input.

I propose that we look at business growth in terms of a model and a customer experience, as opposed to the development of a single product or service.

Earlier we used the words "disruptive entrepreneur" and now let us build on that a bit. The innovator in business is the person who is adept at creative disruption.

Learning how to be different is a skill like all the others. It is about challenging conventions and breaking the rules but more than that it is about redefining your market in a different way.

For example, it is about considering how applying new technology would impact the delivery of your service or the creation of your product. It is about considering changing trends in consumer behavior and how you could move to make the most of them to connect more people to your business.

It is about finding new revenue streams built around strong new value propositions and a better business model.

The new buzzword for innovative thinkers is "design thinking" and that's a good way to describe it since today more than ever you need insight to understand the real motivation and goals of your customers. You can augment your personal observations with analytics and intuition. By gathering more information, you can better define challenges in the market and find opportunities to provide solutions.

Finally, you have to do all of this on mental steroids. The innovative mindset means accelerating the pace from idea to action to implementation. You have to think leanly and have a disciplined implementation process, or you will miss your chance in our rapid-fire times of change.

So how do you develop this innovative power that you need to prosper as you grow your business?

Here are eight characteristics that will heighten your innovative mindset:

BE A PROBLEM FINDER

That's right. The world is full of problem solvers. The trick in being truly innovative is to be able to discern the problems that other people don't see and then solve them.

To be a problem finder you have to ask great questions. When you are with your clients, for example, instead of always pushing your agenda on them find out what situation is really bothering them, no matter how insignificant or impossible it seems.

Innovation begins by finding the right question, not the right answer.

PAY ATTENTION TO THE DETAILS OF THE WORLD AROUND YOU

Wherever you are, be conscious of your surroundings. Even if the scene is one you have seen a hundred times, note the details and if anything has changed.

The innovative person is constantly checking all the things in their world and creating connections. Keep a notebook in your pocket or a mobile app on your phone that lets you record thoughts, ideas and images that strike you as something you need to consider later.

There is wisdom just waiting to be found all around us, but most of us are too busy with our predetermined agendas to notice it.

YOUR TO-DO LIST NEEDS TO HAVE A DONE-THIS COMPONENT

For an entrepreneur with an innovative mindset it is not enough to fill each day with a series of accomplishments.

As satisfying as it feels to study a to-do list and see everything accomplished, it will help more to schedule time each day to look over the list and consider those things that were done and if they were done effectively.

What really worked well, and what didn't? What was a struggle? Why was it a struggle?

Ask yourself: "What did I build today that I could build upon tomorrow?"

If you are a doer, you will accomplish much. But it is only when you schedule the time to reflect on what you have done that you give innovation time to percolate.

HONE YOUR SENSE OF EMPATHY

We often say that innovation is a process of finding solutions, but the big question we need to be truly inspired is to ask ourselves who those solutions are for.

To find better ways of doing things, it is important to have a vision in your mind of the customer you are helping. What is best for them?

That means that you have to have a deep understanding of their experiences with your products and services and immerse yourself in what you do from their perspective. You need empathy.

You need to put yourself in your customer's shoes before you can create solutions that wow them.

REMEMBER THAT THE INNOVATIVE ENTREPRENEUR IS ALSO A CREATOR

Having great ideas is just a small part of business growth, as vital as these ideas are.

But your ideas will never work if you can't bring them to fruition through your hard work.

You need to discuss them and consider them and reflect on them. Then you have to take action and implement them.

That is how good ideas become great ideas for your company.

DEVELOP A RESILIENT MINDSET

Moving hand in hand with the innovative mindset is the resilient mindset. In business and in life, often things do not go entirely as you planned. Your first attempts may not be successful. Innovators do not give up on the road to executing their great ideas.

Remember that 12 publishers rejected J. K. Rowling's first *Harry Potter* book. Resilience was all she had at that time as a penniless single mom.

Walt Disney's first animation company went bankrupt.

Twenty-seven publishers rejected Theodore Seuss Geisel's first children's book, the classic we all know now as *The Cat in the Hat* by Dr. Seuss.

And Steven Spielberg was twice denied entrance to the prestigious University of Southern California film school he wanted to attend. So he went to Cal State instead and went on to movie greatness.

NETWORK LIKE YOUR BUSINESS DEPENDS ON IT

As Steven Johnson so eloquently put it, "chance favors the connected mind."

Today's collaborative workplaces are idea spaces for ideas to be shared and improved upon. If you work alone, take time to build strong networks of people whose opinion you respect and from whom you can learn.

Innovators are traditionally not the lone genius who locks himself or herself in the lab and shuns all human contact. Instead, they are social entrepreneurs who share concepts and ideas and build them through a series of informal feedback exercises with others.

We live in the best era yet for networking, thanks to the advent of social media. On sites like LinkedIn you can connect with industry groups and gather intelligence and share your thoughts to learn how others are responding.

DON'T BE AFRAID TO TAKE RISKS

The killer to innovation is the attitude that "we tried this once and it didn't work" or "this is how we do things here."

Process is good, and in fact, process and systems are necessary in any business to achieve a high level of efficiency.

But when it comes to developing new ideas into products and services, sometimes you have to go down different roads and abandon what you have always done.

You need to try something different as you build on your failures. To innovate, it is as vital to know what doesn't work as to know what does.

The true innovative mindset allows you to change with a purpose, to search with joy to see different things and to interpret them uniquely.

INCORPORATE INNOVATION INTO YOUR WORK PLAN

Now you have some insight into the innovative mind, the next challenge is to find that balance between innovating and adding new products and services to your offerings, and keeping production steady and customers satisfied on a day to day basis.

That is a massive challenge when you work as a solopreneur or with a very small team.

As with so many things, it is all about balance. Just as you create times and places for production of your daily work, you need to schedule in periods to look for and develop new ideas.

The difficult thing to understand about innovation is that it isn't just that lightning bolt idea as we said at the beginning of this lecture. Instead, it is a process of innovation that rides along side by side with you excelling at all the things you are already doing well in your business.

Want to develop a new service? You know you can't just shut down what you do for a whole week or month and focus on it. But you can say that you will take every Tuesday morning to develop that product.

Can a free spirit of innovation be confined to such a schedule? Actually it can. Remember, it doesn't mean that you can't be thinking about what you are going to do that is different on a regular basis several times a day.

It is a myth to think that you can "make" your company innovative as if by announcing it to your staff it will suddenly happen. Innovation is not a distinct thing that is divorced from your day-to-day excellence. It is something that happens simultaneously with it.

It's like mashed potatoes and gravy. The two go together, but the gravy goes on top of the mashed potatoes, not underneath it. Innovation goes on top of what you are already doing that is good.

But the reason I suggest scheduling some thinking time for innovation is that if you don't you tend to get caught up totally in the activity of your work and not in the thinking about it, not in asking the "what if" questions, not in considering "this is good, but could it be better?" questions.

Innovation can be as simple as a course correction. A project is launched and going smoothly, but it lacks the wow factor. A quick session to consider what else could be done to take it to the next level may yield the answers you are seeking.

ONE GOOD EXAMPLE OF INNOVATION AT WORK

A great example of how one company exhibits a great innovation mindset in action is to look at 3M Corporation.

Their management defines innovation as the ability for their employees to see and act on opportunities, to maintain a laser focus on outcomes and to avoid getting caught in the activity trap.

What they do in particular is to send scientists out into the field to observe customers and understand their pain points. Customers are also invited inside to Innovation Centers to explore possibilities for solving problems and generating new product ideas. Meanwhile, employees are also given a chance to go into innovation centers and create a pool of practical ideas that can be nurtured.

One thing they are keen on is maintaining a critical balance between present and future issues. Staying on top of new trends and innovating cannot hinder day to day production, but they find a way to blend it all together.

The way they do this is to employ what they call "The Thirty Percent Rule."

That means that for each department, thirty percent of their revenue must come from products introduced in the last four years. They track this rigorously and employee bonuses hinge on ensuring this goal is attained.

They build their great innovation success (like Post-It notes, for example) into the story of the corporate culture, so that each new generation of employees can be inspired. They set up a series of structures and systems that allows for new ideas to be explored and developed. They tolerate mistakes.

In addition to their Thirty Percent Rule, they have a Fifteen Percent Rule. That means that 3M's engineers and scientist can spend up to fifteen percent of their own time pursuing projects of their own choice, free to look for unexpected, unscripted opportunities for breakthrough innovations that can expand the pie.

One of the results was the invention of the first electronic stethoscope with Bluetooth technology that allows doctors to listen to a patient's heart and lung sounds as they go on their rounds, transferring the data to software programs for deeper analysis.

The board chairman William McKnight explained the importance of the fifteen percent free time rule by saying "If you put fences around people, you get sheep. Give people the room they need."

So don't be a sheep.

Think about how you can build your own winning mindset and spend time next month considering what new ways you can innovate for the benefit of your company.

THE CONQUER ZONE

Do you have an innovative mindset? Answer these three questions honestly.

Question #1. What is the most innovative thing you have ever done in your company?

Question #2. What made it so innovative and did it work?

Question #3. List three innovative ideas you would like to explore in the next month that could take your business to a new level.

ENERGIZER

"The only way you survive is you continuously transform into something else. It's the idea of continuous transformation that makes you an innovative company."

- Ginni Rometty

CHAPTER SEVEN

HOW TO STAY BALANCED BETWEEN RISK AND OPPORTUNITY

TRADITIONALLY, WHEN WE look at revenue growth our focus is on revenue. It seems like a no-brainer.

In this chapter, I want to explore another way of coming at the issue of revenue growth.

That is by focusing on profits instead over overall revenue.

There is an old business joke that says "We lose money on every sale, but we'll make it up on volume."

Yes, it is funny, but it is also sad.

Many entrepreneurs hitting the fast-lane button to growth suddenly discover that it is much harder to make a profit than it is to create something or sell something.

That's because no matter what the nature of your business is, you have a series of fixed costs. Even if you work in a home office, you have to pay for your Internet connection, your lights, heat, office supplies, computers and printers, and support services.

For many people who build their business around offering a service they almost randomly pick an amount that they feel their time is worth assuming that since they work at home, they have virtually no overhead.

They forget the cost of filling their car with gas to go to meetings and maintaining the vehicle. They forget the cost of purchasing their business suit, and of getting their presentation printed. They forget the time lost in a series of short phone calls and the series of meetings they attended with a variety of clients before they secured their jobs.

Because of that, they think of their revenue growth as the number of hours they worked and the fee they were able to charge. They calculate the revenue only, forgetting to factor in the full costs of creating that revenue.

When you take the price of your fixed costs from your revenue figure, that's when you come up with your profit figure.

And when it comes to seriously knowing where you stand as you prepare to grow your business, that is a crucial fact to know.

A friend of mine experienced this discrepancy of numbers at a young age when she decided to run an ice cream stand during the summer to raise funds for university. She secured a source for the ice cream at a fixed price, some freezer space, and a shed on property her father owned. He did not charge her rent.

Based on these factors, she priced her ice cream and anticipated her revenue.

But at the end of the summer, as she calculated her revenue, it did not match the profit she had anticipated.

That is because she forgot to factor into her ice cream price the cost of the municipal permit to operate her business, the cost of her posters and advertising, and the cost of her lights.

Your fixed costs take a significant chunk out of your dollars earned.

That's what made her develop this new formula, which has served her well in the business world.

The formula and philosophy is simply that growth is about creating profits, not revenue.

In simple terms, if you shift your sights today from revenue growth to profit growth, you will focus more clearly on all the right things.

I have seen it happen time and again.

Anyone operating in a competitive marketplace can increase their revenue by cutting their price or offering a special promotion. But these actions in themselves never lead to profitable growth in the long term. What you are doing is sacrificing your margin of profit to increase your revenue. It is not sustainable.

That is why it is so important to be able to accurately

estimate the likely return on investment from every growth initiative that you make.

How do you know what you should be investing in then?

You should be investing in initiatives that improve your competitive position in your marketplace. If you are not, even if you do everything else right, you will gradually see your competitive position erode and you will watch in dismay as your revenue starts to decline.

To give you a real-life example of how this formula works, consider a company like Gatorade. In the 1970s it was just a small business but it had a great idea and gradually, it grew and grew as it sold more Gatorade. But instead of just growing its revenue, it also continued to grow its profits and it re-invested some of those profits into the aggressive upkeep and promotion of its brand. By the 1990s, it was a billion dollar business, but it still consistently watched its profits, and re-invested in its brand, no matter how much its revenue grew.

That proved to be their survival cushion when Coca-Cola decided to compete with it by launching a similar product called Powerade. Even though they suddenly had an impressive competitor, they could continue to build revenue because they maintained such a powerful brand presence.

When you create healthy profits and you re-invest

some of them consistently to grow and strengthen your company, you become almost impossible to beat. If you increase revenue just for the sake of increasing revenue, of looking good on the next quarter's spreadsheet delivered to your investors, you will rarely achieve the long-term success that you need to survive.

The question is, how can you determine the best formula for growing profits in your business? You need a formula that will help you consistently see an increasing level of bottom line growth.

This formula brings together a lot of components. In fact, to get your profit margins right, you need to multiply five key facts about your business.

The first is the number of leads you follow each year. How many people do you put into your sales funnel?

The second, is to figure out from your total number of leads how many people actually buy something? If ten people enter your sales funnel each day, and three of them on average buy something, then you can say the figure for your conversion rate is three out of ten, or thirty percent.

The third, is to figure out how much your customers spend for each sale. It might be as little as five dollars if you are selling small products, or it might be tens of thousands of dollars if you are selling consulting services or homes or cars.

Fourth, determine the average number of purchases of goods or services the average customer makes in any given year. This will be an estimate, of course.

Fifth and finally, estimate the profit percentage of every sale you make. For example, if you sell a product or service for $100, and your profit is $25, then your profit margin is twenty-five percent.

In a blog published on the Entrepreneur site a few years ago, contributor, Brad Sugars, took these numbers and showed how effectively they could be used to help you plan your expansion strategy.

He puts it like this:

You are running a business that converts one out of four prospects in your sales funnel into paying customers.

Those customers pay an average of $100 for each purchase, and they usually purchase two items a year.

Your company has a twenty-five percent profit margin, so that means you are currently experiencing revenues of $200,000 a year.

Your total profit for the year, however, is $50,000.

Want to grow your company now?

What would happen if over the next year you increased your results by just ten percent in each of the five areas we discussed?

Your 1,000 customers would become 1,210 customers.

Their average $100 purchases would become $110 purchases and they would be making them 2.2 times a year. That means your revenue would suddenly go up from $200,000 to $292,820.

As a result, your profit of twenty-seven point five percent on a revenue of $292,820 would hike up from $50,000 a year to $80,525.

That's a perfect example of what happens in your company when you focus on profit instead of revenue as you grow.

Your new bottom line looks fascinating, doesn't it? By just increasing each factor in your profit generating formula by only ten percent, you could see your profit go up sixty-one percent in one year, for a total of $30,525.

Couldn't you use an extra $30,000 a year in your business?

Imagine what would happen if you were able to increase each factor by even more, like fifteen percent or twenty percent or even one-hundred percent.

What makes this an accurate prediction of growth is that you are multiplying all the factors of growth, not just adding them. It is a new way to look at business growth and work with numbers that every company, not matter how small, can produce.

It is the best explanation I have seen on this subject.

If you grow in this way, you will be amazed by your success.

You will sit there, putting more people into your sales funnel at the start of each year and carefully nursing them through to their sales. Your competitors, meanwhile, will be out there slashing their expenses, offering special promotions that lower their profit margins even while increasing their revenue, and spinning their wheels without any real growth.

The bottom line is that growing your business is all about getting good leads, encouraging your customers once they start buying from you to buy more and buy more often and raising your profit margins.

If you do that, your revenue will grow and your profits will grow and your business will be stable.

So how do you start this formula working for you?

It all starts with getting more customers into your sales funnel and getting your current customers to buy more.

THE CONQUER ZONE

It is time to ignite your mental calculator.

You need to do some soul-searching as you consider your profits, as opposed to your revenue.

Grab a pen and paper or electronic notebook and answer these questions about your core company.

1. How many leads do you follow each year?

2. How many people do you put into your sales funnel?

3. How many of the people in your sales funnel actually buy a product or service from you?

4. On average, what do they spend with each purchase?

5. How many items do they purchase on average each year? (This will be an estimate.)

6. What is the profit margin on each sale you make?

7. What would happen if you increased your results by just ten percent in each of the categories?

When you are done with your calculations, join in a group discussion while you share whether or not you could increase your financial picture by focusing on profits, not just revenue. How will it change your approach to business?

ENERGIZER

"The buyer is entitled to a bargain. The seller is entitled to a profit. So there is a fine margin in between where the price is right. I have found this to be true to this day whether dealing in paper hats, winter underwear or hotels."

– Conrad Hilton

CHAPTER EIGHT

HOW TO DELIGHT YOUR CUSTOMERS

"If you do build a great experience, customers tell each other about that. Word of mouth is very powerful."

- Jeff Bezos

CUSTOMER SERVICE IS about one thing and one thing only.

That is trust.

Trust is what makes people buy your product, believe in your promises and warranties, and engage with your brand.

It is the single biggest element you need to consider when you look at growing your business by attracting new customers and keeping your current ones.

The problem is that building trust with your customers and maintaining that trust is no longer as simple as having a good formula, reliable production and excellent delivery methods.

It used to be, but it isn't anymore.

In fact, the digital age in which you are attempting to grow your business has so completely changed who and what people trust and why they trust that the rules on how we grow our business are turned upside down.

People no longer blindly trust their institutions and government. Every single person with access to the Internet can review your company in the harshest possible terms.

The new kind of trust is when two people, who have no logical reason to trust each other (mainly because they don't know each other at all), decide to trust each other because a third party has put them together. In business, this is called a referral.

This is the most powerful governing trust in the digital age.

This changing perception of trust related to customer service started very simply.

It started with a token of trust, a credit card. You pay for goods with a credit card. The cashier accepts that through the swipe of your plastic strip, the business will receive the money you owe. The bank granting you the credit card accepts that you will pay the money owed each month. Technology has made this all possible.

That was very, very early in the digital age. All you needed was a trusted third party in the equation, in this case VISA or MasterCard or American Express, and presto, you had trust.

But the digital age has gotten much more complicated and turned the trust equation upside down again.

Social media gave customers a new vehicle to drive their business transactions. They realized they didn't have to rely on just one single third party, like VISA, as a trust facilitator. They discovered that by going on social media and asking a question about your company's service or product, they could unleash a whole bunch of opinions about whether or not you could be trusted. They also assumed, naively perhaps, that they could consider the opinions shared as unbiased and trustworthy. Most of them still think that.

We moved from the institutional or organizational trust of the Industrial Age through to the third party trust of the early Computer Age into the full concept of peer trust in the Digital Age.

This is important to you because now when you look at growing your business and securing new customers and keeping current ones, you have to be conscious of the impact of peer trust.

Examples of mega companies that thrive because of peer trust are Uber, Airbnb, and VRBO (Vacation Rentals by Owners). These companies have to be run bottom-up, not top-down. They are decentralized and democratic.

What does this mean to your business?

It means that the customers who will hire you for your services or buy your products in the future will not necessarily do that because of your standing with the Chamber of Commerce, or the number of corporate boards you sit on, or the scholarly standing you achieved from your university.

Instead, they will hire you more likely because their brother-in-law got good service from you, or their hair stylist thought you did a good job, or the small business owner you counselled told his colleagues you helped him.

With all the voices that will be heard about the value of your products or services, your business growth model has suddenly become more complex. You have to grow your business person by person, not, necessarily, target by target.

Think about what this really means.

When I was a child, my parents repeatedly reminded me never to get into a car driven by strangers, no matter how much candy was offered.

They made me promise this.

They also made me promise to make sure that, as a teenager, I kept the door of our home locked when they were out. No strangers were to be allowed to enter our home in their absence.

They reminded me that it was not safe to trust people I did not know.

But now, as a culture, we rent rooms in our homes to strangers, we jump into cars driven by people who don't even have a basic taxi license, and we give our cash to contractors who apparently did a good job for our cousin's neighbor's friend!

Business growth has suddenly become a very unwieldy, message proposition and it is likely to remain that way for a few more years. The risks of each customer engagement now are higher, the push for complete accountability higher, and the cost of upsetting a customer could be very high indeed.

This is our new reality. This is what we need to work with and determine strategies to overcome.

Consumer relationships are now a high stakes game. One happy customer can touch hundreds and even thousands of other potential customers for you. One unhappy customer can do the same. What people think of you and your business is no longer based on your Better Business Bureau ranking. Your reputation depends on the person walking down any street in any town.

How did this happen? Can we change it? Can we make it work for us?

It happened because people lost faith that their governments and institutions and corporations had their best interests at heart. It happened because people believed that all of these big institutions existed to serve their own interests first, and line their own pockets, and forget about quality and value and caring for their customers and constituents.

It happened because people became disillusioned. So they turned away from nameless, faceless big businesses and turned back to trusting themselves and the information they could ferret out for themselves.

How do you grow your business in this climate and delight your customers?

You grow by building trust in your reputation.

You do this by sharing with a generous spirit and open heart.

You do this by caring about your customers and showing them that they matter to you as individuals.

You do this by building relationships with them.

Building trust happens on the foundation of your attitude towards your clients. It happens because you understand the fragility of all relationships and understand that they can't be taken for granted.

Building trust requires that you are respectful to your employees, your partners, your suppliers, your community and of course, your customers. You need to find time to court your customers and show the human side of your business.

To illustrate how this new approach works, let's take a look at this story from Shep Hyken, now a well-known service engagement guru who teaches people how to create loyal customers who will spread trust about their company. In fact, Shep carries the title CAO of Shephard Presentations, by which he means Chief Amazement Officer.

He tells this story about a job he had back in his college days, well before he built the amazing speaking and coaching business he has today.

"One very, very cold day...a woman got out of the car to pump gas, an elderly woman," he says. "I went out and pumped her gas for her. My manager got upset with me for pumping this lady's gas. He says, 'we're a self-serve station' and I thought, well, you know, 'but she could have died, slipped on a piece of ice. I mean, she looked frail.' So I helped her and he says, 'What is she going to do the next time? She's going to expect the same thing.' And I said, 'well, that's fine because there's three other stations, one on each of the corners (of) the intersection, and I think that I'd love her to come back and always do business with us'."

Hyken's point is that it's okay to build your customer's expectations that they will receive extraordinary service and care from you. Let them trust that you will treat them better than any of your competitors.

I have already made the point that you cannot compete on price alone. Customer service is what matters most, and that is more important than ever because of the way changing perceptions of trust and mass access to social media has changed the world.

There has never been a point in history when customers have had a bigger voice than now. This raises the bar for you to become more effective in ensuring those voices are raised in a chorus of praise.

You need to be respectful and responsive to your customers, always getting back to them quickly and courteously, no matter how difficult it may be.

Most of all, you need to be able to maintain a conversation with them.

That conversation generally takes place on social media. It is vital that you engage respectfully with your customers and build trusting relationships. They need to know that you are there with equal commitment when everything is good and when things go wrong.

Social media isn't a threat to your business if you get the basics right, offline and online, all the time.

That is the challenge for all of us as entrepreneurs growing our business.

To meet that challenge, I suggest that you start to focus on the whole customer experience, not just customer service as we did in previous generations.

Let me explain the difference.

If you contact a travel agency and book a trip and the person you deal with on the phone or at the office is friendly and helpful and helps you purchase the best vacation for you, then you have had good customer service.

But if you leave the office, and your tickets arrive earlier than expected, if when you arrive at the hotel the agent has secured an upgrade for you, if your car rental arrives and it is even nicer than you expected, and if the local tour guide the agent recommended is amazing, then you have moved past customer service into a great customer experience.

When you have a great customer experience, you are inspired to tell your friends about it in person and on social media. You are even inspired to write a glowing review and put it on the travel agent's website. You might even go so far as to call the agent upon your return and for sure, the next time you want to get away, you will go back to that agency and that agent who served you.

In that one experience, you become loyal to that company and freely gave of your services to be their ambassador.

Customer experience isn't just one transaction between your business and your customer. It is more like the series of interactions between your business and your customer throughout your entire business relationship.

Businesses that deliver an amazing customer experience don't do it by a fluke. They have a thoughtful, written and followed customer experience strategy that doesn't leave anything to chance.

Why does this matter to your company?

There are a great many benefits of giving a great customer experience, not the least of which, your customers keep coming back.

Additionally, according to research done by American Express, sixty percent of customers overall are willing to pay more for a product or service when it delivers a great customer experience.

So, it impacts your bottom line as well as your repeat business. In fact, the happier you are with a company, the longer you stay with them. Conversely, the more frustrated you are, the more likely you are to leave.

Your business cannot exist and prosper without customers. You need your current customers to come back and you need new customers as well. Again, that's where great customer experiences can benefit your company, because the easiest way to draw in a new customer is on a recommendation from a current customer.

In 2015, Watermark Consulting did a Customer Experience Return on Investment Study to demonstrate the actual business value of providing a great customer experience. To do this, they studied the cumulative total stock returns for two model portfolios ...one was the Top Ten Leaders and the other the Bottom Ten Laggards of publicly traded companies in Forrester Research's annual Customer Experience Index ratings.

They discovered that companies who led in the great customer experience delivery outperformed the broader market, generating a total return that was 35 points higher than the S&P 500 Index.

I wanted to talk about this study because this particular analysis reflects nearly a decade of performance results. That means it spans one total economic cycle, from the pre-recession market peak in 2007 to the post-recession recovery that continues today. The results were consistent, despite the economic times. Delivering a great customer experience significantly impacts the value of your company.

Delving deeper into the study, I discovered that the leaders had better customer retention, less price sensitivity, greater wallet share, and positive word-of-mouth.

They also had lower expenses because they had fewer complaints to deal with and less intense service requirements demanded by unhappy customers.

The laggards had higher operating expenses because they had to deal with increased attrition and negative word-of-mouth issues.

Companies who lagged in the customer experience delivery area trailed far behind, posting a total return that was 45 points lower than that of the broader market.

So you know what you need to deliver this great customer experience ...that's easy to figure out.

What is not easy is to determine what it is within your business that will turn a customer's experience from ordinary to great.

I am not making this up; research shows this is a real problem for all businesses.

Bain & Company asked businesses and organizations to rate the quality of their customer experience and the executives at eighty percent of the companies surveyed said they were delivering a really superior customer experience. They were pleased with themselves.

Then Bain & Company asked customers to rate their customer experience, and the customers said only eight percent of the companies were delivering a great customer experience.

There's a pretty big gap between eighty and eight.

And this is not the only survey to show that most

companies have a problem perceiving how what they offer is viewed by their customers.

In Temkin Group's 2016 Customer Experience Rating Survey, the researchers picked up a severe decline in customer experience. In 2015, for example, customers identified good and excellent customer experiences to be delivered by thirty-seven percent of the companies they dealt with that year. Just one year later, in 2016, this satisfaction rate dropped from thirty-seven percent to only eighteen percent.

That's the lowest rating for great customer experiences since 2011.

Think about it. How is this happening at a time when we have never had more technological tools to tell us what consumers want?

How is this happening at a time when we have never had so many voices on social media telling us what is good and what is bad?

How is this happening where there are so many venues where we can speak to our customers and gain feedback from them?

How is this happening?

It is happening because we are not paying attention. We are not listening to these voices of our customers. We are not conscious that what they wanted last year may not be what they want this year.

So, you have to go back to what really constitutes a great customer experience and how you can provide it. You have to dissect it and pull out its parts so we can learn how to put them all back together again. And then you have to figure out how you can make it even better.

The big question is, what do the top leaders in delivering a great customer experience do differently from everyone else?

Going back to the Watermark Consulting study, there were five key factors that distinguished the best from the others:

1. They aimed for more than customer satisfaction. They didn't aim just to please, they aimed to delight.

2. They nailed down the basics and then delivered pleasant surprises. As children we love happy surprises, as adults we love them just as much.

3. They understood that great customer experiences are intentional and emotional. These leading companies left nothing to chance. They identified emotional touchpoints and connected with them.

4. They shaped customer impressions through cognitive science. These leading companies managed both the reality and the perception of their customer experience. They understood

how the human mind interprets experiences and forms memories.

5. Finally, they recognize the link between the customer and the employee experience. Happy, engaged employees help create happy, loyal customers (who in turn create more happy, engaged employees).

Interestingly enough, Watermark Consulting's research led them to their own philosophy which I will share with you, because it may be one of the most effective customer experience strategies I've ever heard.

This is it.

They believe that with every interaction, businesses win or lose share. Each touchpoint, be it with customers, distributors, or even employees, presents an opportunity to either build brand loyalty or erode it.

Here's another example. This one is from Zappos. Their customer experience strategy is: Deliver "wow" through service, be humble and embrace change. Everything they do is driven by that vision.

How will you create your own customer experience strategy for your company?

Start with a vision of what your best customer experience will look like.

To do that you must know who your customers are. Where do they live? What is their average income? Do they have families and spend a lot of time with their families? What do they do when they are not working? What kinds of work do they do? There is no detail too big or too small to be ignored as you gather data about your customers.

Once you have your data, build a customer avatar that you can share with your employees so they will better understand the person they are dealing with.

The third step is to build an emotional connection with your customers.

Earlier I mentioned Zappos. Let me tell you what Zappos did to build an emotional connection. They had a customer who was late returning a pair of shoes because her mother had died. When she called to advise her customer service representative what had happened, Zappos took care of the return shipping and had a courier pick up the shoes without cost.

Nice touch, wasn't it? Pretty impressive? But they didn't stop there.

The next day the customer arrived home to find a bouquet of flowers with a note from the Zappos customer service team who sent their condolences.

Remember, according to the Journal of Consumer Research, more than fifty percent of an experience is based on emotion and emotions shape the customer's attitude. If you can connect in a special way with a customer you have built a force more powerful than you can imagine.

Here's some other examples of companies who really "get it" when it comes to amazing customer experiences.

Trader Joe's in the United States ended up with an amazing reputation and a rush of Christmas business after a happy customer shared the story of her excellent customer experience with them.

The customer was a woman who was worried about her father, an 89-year-old man from Pennsylvania who was snowed in just before the holidays and was running out of food. The daughter, who didn't live near her father, called many stores to see if they would deliver to the elderly man, but none would.

She finally heard about Trader Joe's and called to tell them her story. They said they don't normally deliver, but they would make an exception in this instance.

The customer service representative took the time to help the woman create a list and even suggested some items that would fit the man's special low-sodium diet.

The daughter ordered around $50 worth of food to be delivered. She was a happy customer when she was advised the food would be taken to the man.

Then Trader Joe's upped the emotional connection and turned the experience from good to amazing.

The employee told the lady that she didn't have to pay for the food, and to have a Merry Christmas. The food was delivered within thirty minutes of the phone call and the holidays were saved for the old man and his family.

The good emotions this stirred up in other customers when the story was told was priceless.

A Harvard Business Review study shows us that customers who are emotionally connected to our companies are three times more likely to recommend our product or service, they are three times more likely to re-purchase, they are less likely to shop around, and they are much less price sensitive.

If you form your own customer experience strategy today and you follow it, how do you know for sure that it is working for you?

The best way is to ask for customer feedback in real time, as in right after the interaction with your company. You can send surveys via email or calls. If you have several employees, it's a good idea to tie the excellent customer experience to the one particular employee who may have handled it. That way it is rewarding for them and inspiring for others.

Have a formalized system to analyze feedback and then act on it to stay in tune with your customers.

Remember that customer experience is a part of

your business that requires constant nurturing. But it is worth the time it takes since in the end you will have increased customer loyalty, higher retention and increased revenues.

THE CONQUER ZONE

Spend the next ten minutes considering a picture of who your customers really are.

What do they do for a living or a hobby? What do they do when they are not working? Where do they live? Do they have families? What emotional triggers do they have that would make them happy?

Create a full customer avatar.

Now consider what that customer would connect with emotionally. What would make their interactions with your company special?

ENERGIZER

"The more you engage with customers the clearer things become and the easier it is to determine what you should be doing."

– John Russell

CHAPTER 9

HOW YOU CAN BE SURE YOU ARE MAKING THE RIGHT DECISION

"Whenever you see a successful business, someone once made a courageous decision."

– Peter Drucker

T O FIND THE COURAGE to start your own business and to get to the top of other businesses in your work experience, you needed to be able to take risks and exhibit confidence and decisiveness.

These are qualities greatly admired in the business world.

People who are timid, less sure that what they are doing is the correct way to go, and more collaborative in approach rarely make it to the top positions.

It is just the way our business culture is set up.

It is not cool for us to acknowledge our own biases, so we hide them under a rock and say what we think needs to be said. Nobody wants to admit that they have any biases. It is an ugly word linked to ugly behavior. So, we delude ourselves.

As our companies grow we have to make more and more decisions. We are strong, we are powerful so, we have to make our own decisions.

We do that by digging into our own experiences more often than we extend ourselves outward.

You see examples of entrepreneurs and managers using their experience as a key focus point of decision making all the time.

The best example I can think of is when you decide to do your budget for next year. What's the first thing you reach for? Your last year's budget. Don't worry, so does everyone else.

At one point in my own career I ventured into a business that I believed had great potential. I tried to build it the way I built all my other businesses, but it didn't fit the same mold. I reverted to doing what I had always done, but things didn't work as I needed them to.

I had to endure a failure to realize that basing everything on my past experiences wasn't the best solution. Had I looked from a different perspective earlier in the process, I would have done things differently.

Making smart decisions is one of the toughest parts of growing your business. To do that, we need an effective process for decision-making. But how do we devise that? What works and what doesn't?

Let's start by looking at two words that you hear a lot today in business that sound good, but fall short of pushing us to make great decisions.

The words we hear are "best practices." If we can deliver services by "best practices," if we can make decisions by "best practices" and if we can create new products using "best practices," then we should be doing okay, shouldn't we?

Not necessarily.

Remember what best practices really means. It means of all the things that have been done before these practices were the best so we will make them our baseline to go forward.

A less positive way to consider best practices is that best practices are past practices. The danger with them is that while they may have been "best" when they were first conceived, the pace of change in today's business world means they may no longer be best at all.

And adherence to these practices as a method of making decisions could be discouraging your team members from rebelling against these practices and giving you new insight about what could work better.

At the same time, innovative companies shy away from suggestions that decision-making could be more effective if it was a process. The word process implies a slow-moving bureaucracy that lumbers along, wresting with all the ins and outs of an issue, until so much time has passed that the issue is no longer even relevant and all chance of seizing an opportunity is gone.

Paul Nutt, author of the thought-provoking book called *Why Decisions Fail*, tells us that half of the decisions made in organizations fail, making failure far more prevalent than we thought.

Furthermore, that failure can be directly linked to the actions of decision makers.

Paul is a professor of management sciences and public policy and management in Fisher College of Business at Ohio State University. The basis for his book involves his critiques of fifteen infamously bad decisions that became public debacles.

What he found was that there are three common blunders made in all horrible decisions:

» Managers and entrepreneurs rush to judgment and make premature commitments.

» They misuse resources.

» They apply failure-prone tactics.

After reading Paul's book I became convinced that we spend too little time thinking about how to make a decision without getting help in identifying what does and what does not work. Because of that, widespread use of failure-prone practices continues.

There is a great tendency for all of us to jump on the first idea that comes along and spend years trying to make it work. Fed by ego and fear of the unknown, we seek self-gratification by sticking to our decisions and trying to prove they are valid.

We often hear ourselves and others saying: "Why re-invent the wheel?" as we settle for an easy way out. That is seductive and deceiving. When we say that, we are really saying that we are not interested in seeing if there is a better way to move vehicles forward.

Paul's research also showed that the number of alternative decisions that leadership teams consider in seventy percent of all important strategic decisions is exactly one.

Despite that, there is a lot of evidence that suggests that if you get a second alternative, your decisions will increase dramatically.

So, how do you change the way you make decisions so that you will make better ones?

Olivier Sibony of McKinsey & Company once remarked that what his company did was to always ask people making an investment recommendation to present their second-best choice as well as their first. He acknowledged that the second choice might not be any better than the first, but both might actually be good and should be considered. In other instances, neither one might not hold up as well as another business unit's choices.

In a conversation with Stanford University Professor and author Chip Heath that was transcribed and published in the McKinsey Quarterly four years ago, Olivier said when people ask him what will make their decision-making process better, he cites three things:

1. First, recognize that very few decisions are one of a kind. You are not the first person in the world to decide to acquire another company or diversify your company. You can learn much from the experiences of others.

2. Recognize uncertainty and have alternatives. Prepare to be wrong and consider a range of outcomes where the worst case is real. It is hard for many decisive entrepreneurs to admit that they are uncertain, but once you acknowledge that, you begin to make headway.

3. Create a debate where people speak up. It's the most obvious thing to suggest that you gather others' opinions, but for many business owners and managers, it is also exceedingly difficult. Your closest team members already have an inkling of the way you are thinking, and it is hard for them to challenge you. But if everyone agrees, you have a group-think situation going on.

In budgeting and planning for the coming year in particular, it is remarkably difficult to break the pattern of bad decision-making. Budgets are dominated by inertia; as soon as you start to build your new budget, as we mentioned, you dig out the old one and work from it. That is not decision-making, it is more a process of anchoring yourself to the past year.

To make better business decisions, you have to find different parameters. You need to focus on what growth will be, not what happened last year. If your budget was 100 last year, maybe it should be 425 this year. Or maybe it should be 87. Take a different viewpoint and be prepared to defend it.

Chip Heath, co-author with his brother, Dan Heath, of the book *Decisive: How to Make Better Decisions in Life and Work,* tells the story of a headhunting firm that did 20,000 executive placements at the C-suite level when it decided to go over its records.

They found that about 40 percent of their recruits were pushed out, failed, or quit within 18 months.

Heath attributed to the shockingly high failure to lots of confirmation biases, such as people who are taller and more attractive do well in interviews, even though those qualities have little to do with the job.

In this case, he suggests that research shows better decisions would be made if Chief Financial Officer candidates were asked to grapple with the financial decisions the company made over the last five years. What would the applicant have thought about, what information would they have collected, and what would they have done?

In other words, make it more like a job sample, not a simple conversation.

One of the reasons entrepreneurs with far less training are successful in business compared to experienced and highly-educated managers is their approach to decision making. The Fortune 5009 manager has to decide whether or not a new product should be introduced. Typically, he or she would run projections from the market data.

But, the entrepreneur is more apt to look away from the data and go find a customer and see if that customer would buy the new product. The entrepreneur is more inclined to experiment and that is a good impulse that leads to better decision-making.

So how do you go about establishing a framework for a good decision making experience?

David Snowden and Mary Boone, in an article called "A Leader's Framework for Decision Making" published in *Harvard Business Review*, suggest that any framework has to overcome three basic problems that plague decision-makers in the business world.

The first is that too many leaders and business owners constantly ask for condensed information. Some will refuse to read more than a page or two of notes on any issue. While this may be a process they find saves them time, it will not save them money if the issue is too complex and cannot be adequately explained in such short order.

Issues that are oversimplified may be handled incorrectly because the key decision-maker is unaware of the intricacies associated with the problem.

Secondly, leaders often succumb to entrained thinking, which is defined as a conditioned response that happens when people become blind to new ways of thinking. These leaders got to the top thinking a certain way, and their framework for all decision making is to retreat to their experience, training and success, instead of considering other options.

When a leader's thinking becomes entrained, they tend to dominate the decision making process. They are inclined to dismiss innovative ideas or solutions by non-experts and this can hurt them in the long run. Entrained thinking can be overcome if you listen to experts, but at the same time, welcome different thoughts from non-experts and consider all solutions put forward.

An example where this worked well was a situation where a shoe manufacturer had pretty much made a decision on a new product, but decided to open up the idea for suggestions from the whole company. A security guard submitted a design for a shoe that became one of the firm's bestsellers.

The third hazard to an effective decision making framework is that when things are going smoothly, many leaders become complacent. If the context suddenly changes, they may react too late because they are seeing what they expect to see, not what is actually happening.

What are some ways you can change the framework for your decision making?

One idea is to take yourself out of your familiar environment and look at the issue from a number of different environments. Think like a customer, think like an employee, think like a non-customer. Walk away from your desk, your chair, your office and go where you see things that you don't see every day. Get out of your comfort zone to clarify and open your thinking.

Introduce game-playing at strategy sessions. This does two things, it moves everyone out of their normal environment and it flattens the hierarchy as managers and staff unite in common goals. Ideas that come out of such arrangements can be fresh and no longer aligned with traditional thinking.

Find ways to reward dissenters and foster a culture where staff members are encouraged to buck the process and avoid group-think. This can be difficult if it is not part of your current leadership style, but it will break down the communication barriers and expose you to more ideas.

Finally, think about your strategy for making decisions in a time of crisis. This is vital to spend a little extra time on because the decisions made under fire can be the ones that literally make or break your company's future.

Nothing defines strong leaders like calm decision-making under crisis in our culture, and yet we must always be aware that works effectively in times of crisis may not translate to times of peace and calm.

A good example was the leadership of then New York Mayor Rudy Giuliani during the Sept. 11 terrorist attack. He immediately showed his effectiveness by making decisions to reestablish order. He was respected.

But when the crisis past, and he continued to make his decision in the same crisis mode, top-down style, he was criticized. His suggestion that elections be postponed to allow him to maintain order and stability fell on deaf ears.

It is still a perfect example to show how one style of decision-making can work really well in one kind of situation (crisis) but is not accepted in different circumstances. Your leadership framework, in other words, needs to be flexible to allow you to switch styles as needed.

A good way to do this is to have parallel frameworks. When chaos reigns, set up a crisis management team that can look at the crisis from various angles and suggest an action that can maintain smooth operations until the waters are calmed. At the same time, set up a parallel team to focus on what can be done in the very near future to benefit from the crisis.

If you delay the second step and wait until everything is calm again, you will miss significant opportunities for growth and for pushing your products and services into a new dimension.

You can see that defining your own decision-making process is not easy. But it will emerge now that you are more aware of patterns and pitfalls of certain decision-making frameworks.

Sometimes you will have to get comfortable voting against yourself.

It is good to understand as well that sometimes you can act on your own, and sometimes it is wiser to share your power and look for wisdom within your group.

The decision- making framework doesn't come in a one-size-fits-all box. What it does come with is no pattern, but just a collection of tools and pieces that you must consider and assemble to meet your own needs.

Sometimes you will build it and have to tear it down and re-assemble it.

Our world is complicated and it is not always easy to put our business problems in context. But now, when you are not in a crisis mode, is the time to consider how you make your decisions about the future of your company and whether or not that is working for you.

THE CONQUER ZONE

Take 10 minutes to think about the best and the worst decision you ever made.

Did you follow the same process in both cases?

What would you do differently now?

ENERGIZER

"And they discovered something very interesting: when it comes to walking, most of the ant's thinking and decision-making is not in its brain at all. It's distributed. It's in its legs.

– Keven Kelly

CHAPTER 10

HOW TO FIND FREEDOM FROM THE TIME MONSTER

"The two most powerful warriors are patience and time."

– Leo Tolstoy

T o HAVE ACCOMPLISHED all that you have in your life so far, you have learned to use your time effectively.

So you may be surprised that I am dedicating a whole chapter on a discussion of time and its impact on you as you work to grow your business.

I am doing this because I discovered that most of the traditional time management programs I have seen do not cover the unique circumstances most entrepreneurs find themselves in on a daily basis.

Your days are far more complex than those of people who go into an office for five days a week and stay there for a set number of hours and then go home to another predictable routine.

So are the roles that you play. You have to move seamlessly from being an accountant, a manager, a coach, a sales professional, a production manager, a performer, a content creator to many other aspects that come from running your own business.

Your motivations are also more complicated than those of many workers. You are not merely working for a pay-check. You need to sustain yourself and your team, but you also need to produce something of value, you need to grow your business, you need time to anticipate trends and interact with your current and prospective customers.

You need time to learn, to create and to plan.

Most entrepreneurs and leaders are also prone to over-committing themselves, forgetting that as they pursue their business dream they also need to find balance to maintain the social contact so vital to keep family and friends feeling valued and important.

And when all those parts of your life are running smoothly, what time have you left for yourself to play? Where are the moments when you can relax or when you can let your imagination run free? When do you take time to fill up your own personal well of energy and resources and imagination?

If you are living life like one massive to-do list, then this lecture is particularly aimed at you. If you have managed to find a better balance, we still hope you will find some new ideas in the next hour that enhance your life.

I'm going to break up this discussion on time into ten realities as it relates to your life.

#1. YOU CANNOT MANAGE TIME.

There are hundreds of books in the marketplace about effective time management.

But you cannot manage time any more than you can manage the wind or the pace of a tree growing. You can channel it and you can nurture it, but it is not a widget that you can create more of if you make some production changes.

It doesn't matter what kind of system you use to keep track of your day. When all is said and done, your day is 24 hours, no more and no less.

You can only manage the choices you make in that day and those choices determine how you spend the specific amount of time you are allotted.

It is your goals that determine how you spend your time. It is your capacity for choice that governs its use.

Time is not hands moving across an antique clock or sand drifting down an hourglass. Time is you, your essence, and the substance of your life.

We love philosopher Amelie Rorty's description of time. She wrote:

"Time is a river which sweeps me along, but I am the river; it is a tiger which destroys me, but I am the tiger; it is a fire which consumes me, but I am the fire."

Despite this, most of us live our lives as if time was an accordion that we can compress and expand at our whim. We delude ourselves by using verbs like "make time," "give time," "take time" or "plunder time."

You don't do any of those things to time. Time is simply the choices that guide your actions over 24-hour periods.

Because of that, your to-do lists are mere dominoes. When one day's task list starts to fall against the other, they collapse into the story of your life. Your lists do not protect you from time's passing; they are time.

#2. WHAT CHOICES WORK BEST FOR YOUR DAY?

If time is about choices, how do you make the choices about spending that time in a way that supports the goals you want to accomplish?

If you fill up your agenda with endless tasks that take every hour of your day but do not propel you closer to your goal for your business and your life, you are working like King Sisyphus, the character from Greek mythology. As a punishment for his self-importance, he was forced every day to role a huge boulder uphill.

At nightfall, he had to push it back down again where it hit him.

The next day, he had to repeat the same futile tasks.

I think most of us worked at some places that felt a lot like that before we became entrepreneurs.

Now we have the choice to make our efforts, our time spent, to move us forward, not run a wheel of useless tasks.

Despite that, a survey done by Tracking Daily Activities reported that thirty-one percent of business executives admitted they wasted one hour daily, while sixteen percent said they wasted two hours. Six percent said they wasted three hours and two percent more wasted between four and five hours.

So how do we ensure that the hours we spent working are bringing us closer to accomplishing what we want?

#3. CHANGE YOUR BEHAVIOR, NOT YOUR SCHEDULE

You can't change time, but you can change your behavior. One of the biggest challenges when we are at work on a project is being interrupted with personal phone calls and texts.

This is a challenge to be sure. You want to cherish the relationships between you and your family and be accessible to them. At the same time, friends can be trained to understand that you don't take personal calls or read texts between 9 and noon, for example.

If they want to invite you somewhere or get a message to you, they can email or message you and you will check it at noon and get back to them then. People who want to meet you for lunch that day will learn to contact you the day before.

Think about this if you don't think your friends can be trained. Right now, I'll bet that some of you know you can't call your friends because it's a certain day at a certain time and that is when they are on dialysis every day, or that is when they are driving a school bus, or that is when they write or paint or do their daily run and they can't be disturbed.

If other people can do it and it doesn't threaten your friendship, why can't you? You can give them a warning and make some arrangement for emergency situations. Otherwise, give yourself this time as a gift and make the most of it.

You can also teach your team members that you accept calls and conferences at certain times of the day but not others. It is your company, after all. They work for you. They will tailor their own work life and uninterrupted work time around yours.

#4. IMPLEMENT A TIME MANAGEMENT PLAN

As an extension of the non-interrupted working time you will start, build on that and start to change even more of your behaviors so you can better get to the goals you want to accomplish. Two big goals that are on most people's lists, that of increasing productivity and reducing stress, both become reachable when you set hours when you can reach a work-flow zone without being interrupted.

What other goals are on your list?

Is your agenda set up to help you accomplish those goals?

Or are you just too busy being busy to get out of a rut?

It is a good idea to make up your task list at the end of your work day just as you are preparing to leave your office.

The next morning, give it a check and note any designated time for meetings or deadlines.

Then look at every task and ask yourself honestly: "Is this getting me closer to the goal I want to achieve?"

If you can't see any connection with what you are doing and the goals you want to achieve, it is really time to redo that list.

You are never going to get to where you want to be if what you are doing isn't leading you there.

#5. KNOW WHAT YOU WANT TO ACHIEVE FROM EACH PHONE CALL AND MEETING

If you go into a meeting without any idea what you want to accomplish, you are having a conversation not a meeting.

There's no harm in having conversations, of course. Sometimes you pick up valuable information or they are personally rewarded. But don't confuse the two.

The same thing goes for phone calls. If you don't know the desired end of the call when you push the call button, you are just calling for a chat.

Take five minutes prior to every phone call and every meeting and jot down what you want to achieve. If you feel yourself getting side-tracked, look at that note and steer the topic back on track.

You need to know what success looks like and sounds like when you go after it or you might miss it.

When each meeting or phone call is done, take five more minutes to figure out whether you got what you wanted. If you did not, why not? Figure it out or it will just keep happening again and again.

Don't be unkind to yourself...this is done as an exercise in learning only.

#6. ACKNOWLEDGE THAT YOU CAN'T GET EVERYTHING ACCOMPLISHED

It is stressful to look at your to-do list at the end of a long and exhausting day and realize that you didn't get everything done.

But if you accept that the items you completed got you closer to your goals then chalk it up as a good day.

Keep in mind the theory that twenty percent of your actions actually produce eighty percent of your results.

#7. LEARN TO DELEGATE AND CONTRACT OUT WORK

If you operate a growing business, and you have not yet learned how important it is for you to delegate tasks to others and secure a team of remote workers who have unique areas of expertise, you will never grow to the extent that you imagine.

That is because there is no one person who can corner all the talent and brains no matter how good you are.

It is so, so difficult for most leaders to give up aspects of control of their business, but outsourcing your accounting, hiring content creators or securing a great sales professional can make all the difference in saving time and achieving greater results.

Sharing the load not only lightens it, but it leaves you free to do what you are best at. The people you contract out to are better at what they do every day as well, and everyone gains in this process.

#8. EDIT YOURSELF CONSTANTLY.

Most of you would never publish a brochure, a book or a blog without editing it ruthlessly.

But every day, every month, and every year you create schedules of what must be done and start applying it to the precious hours of your life without constant editing.

The agenda of how you spend your days is the one thing in your life that demands to be edited more severely than anything else you write.

To approach the editing of yourself take your to-do list and look over each task and ask yourself how you feel about it. Are you eager to start it, or does the very thought of it give you a sinking feeling in the pit of your stomach? Do you want to put that task off for as long as possible?

Highlight every task that you really hate to do.

Make one more cycle through your to-do list. This time look for all the things that are there not because you want to do them, but because you think that you should do them or you feel obligated to do them, or because somebody else expects you to do them. Of themselves, none of these tasks bring you joy.

Highlight all of those tasks as well.

Now assemble all the highlighted tasks.

Delete as many as you reasonably can.

Then delegate as many as you reasonably can.

Such editing will undoubtedly make you anxious, but do it ruthlessly. You are letting go of things that you must release yourself from.

Now look at the remaining, shorter lists of tasks that you still don't want to do.

Rephrase or change them into something that you would enjoy. For example, you may have to collect quotes for paving your driveway or putting a new roof on your house. Couple that task with something you love, like sitting on your deck in the sunshine with a cocktail of your choice. Or head out to your favorite café, find a secluded corner and over your latte make the calls and gather the data, or send emails to relevant suppliers.

With this one exercise, you can succeed in making everything on your to-do list something that brings you joy. Those things are worth investing your time in.

#9. STAY ON TARGET DAILY. COMMITMENT IS KEY.

To stay on top of difficult challenges, and time management is perhaps the most difficult of all challenges; find ways to constantly renew and inspire yourself and your approach to it.

Be strategic and prioritize.

Here are three of my favorite quotations that inspire me to stay on target:

Time management is "a vehicle that can carry you from wherever you are to wherever you want to go." – Brian Tracey, author of *Time Power*

When you delegate activities to others, you "free yourself to focus your time and efforts on those tasks where you can make your best contribution." – Julie Morgenstern, author of *Time Management from the Inside Out*

Work expands to fill the time available. – Northcote Parkinson's Law

#10. NEVER ASK FOR A DEADLINE EXTENSION. IF YOU GET ONE, USE IT WISELY.

When a deadline is extended, we all feel a bit of instant relief.

But research suggests that when deadlines are moved back, most of us do not use the extra time we are given wisely. As the deadline approaches again, we are often in exactly the same state of turmoil that we were the first time.

Psychologically what happens when you get the time extension is that you are increasing the space between you and the finish line. In the space that emerges, other more urgent goals rush in to demand our attention.

We may fool ourselves that it's okay to break our focus now that the pressure is off because foolishly we all believe that we work better under pressure. Few of us actually do. It is under pressure that we get careless, make mistakes, leave gaps in our thinking and produce a completed product, but not our best product.

What we are really saying when we insist that we work better under pressure is that we don't work unless there is pressure on us. And that is a stressful, unhealthful way to work and a bad habit that will ultimately cause you to lose work from clients who are tired of waiting and place undue stress on your body.

How do you cope with the extended deadline and still stay focused on the project?

Set a series of interim deadlines for yourself. This closes the mental gap you have between you and the end of the project. Make sure that these deadlines have a reason attached to them; you are too used to procrastinating if a deadline is not a real deadline.

Better yet, pretend that you didn't hear that the project deadline was extended. Finish it and give yourself a breather afterwards.

THE CONQUER ZONE

Why do you want to manage your time better? (Do you want to earn more money, have more creative seepage time, or spend more time with family and friends, etc.?).

List four reasons that focus on what you want and need more time in your life. Knowing where you stand and what you want is the most powerful tool for change.

Which time management practices work best for you? What am you currently doing right about managing your time?

Which of your time-wasting behaviors do you want to change the most? How are you going to accomplish this?

ENERGIZER

"Let your life lightly dance on the edges of Time like dew on the tip of a leaf."

– Rabindranath Tagore

CHAPTER 11

TELL YOUR STORY BETTER AND LOUDER

"The one thing that you have that nobody else has is you. Your voice, your mind, your story, your vision. So write and draw and build and play and dance and live as only you can."

– Neil Gaiman

EVERY ENTREPRENEUR, visionary or change maker who has ever achieved success began with an idea they believed could be sustainable and a list of what must be done to get it going, along with a sub-list of what would be nice to do if time permitted.

But time just about never pays attention to lists and the second list eventually just falls into the wastebasket and is only heard of again at the dawn of a New Year when it makes a resolution or planning list, and is again ignored.

Sadly, building a strategic communications plan is often on that sub-list.

It is sad, because of all the investments of time and energy you can make in this digital age to fast-track the growth of your business, few are as effective as your communications strategy.

That's because no matter how skilled you are and how awesome your business is, if people don't know about it, they won't buy your goods or services.

Getting your message out to the targeted pool of customers you need is vital. So is portraying yourself as the best option in a competitive marketplace.

If you aren't co-ordinating your marketing brochures with your website, your social media postings with your corporate mission and value system, and your personal elevator remarks with your core strategy, you will waste your efforts and never be quite as effective as you could be with a strategic communications plan.

There is a myth common among many busy entrepreneurs that strategic communications tends to fall into place on its own, as long as you know what you are trying to do and who your customers are.

But that myth is not reality.

You can communicate without a plan, of course. Just opening your mouth and talking about the weather is a way to communicate and perhaps build a bridge between you and a potential customer.

But communication without strategy is just talk.

Strategic communications is about talking with a

purpose and that purpose is to shape the conversation around you and your company.

If you don't have a strategy to tell people who you are, what you do, and what value you offer them, you are leaving it up to them to follow their perception of what they think you are doing and what it might do to help them.

Do you want to take that risk?

Because if you do, and they perceive you as something less than you are, or something of less value than what you offer, you are starting a relationship on ground that is far shakier than if you controlled the message and built it on the firm foundation of your business strategy.

So talk just happens. But strategic communications does not.

Instead, it starts with a plan, it incorporates a system of measuring the effectiveness of that plan, it identifies target audiences, it develops specific messages designed to elicit specific responses from that target audience, and it identifies appropriate channels for your corporate message to be spread.

In building your plan, there is one clear goal and that is to ensure that everything said about you and your company will make it easier for your audience to clearly comprehend the value and benefit that you and your products offer in their lives.

The plan will also give you a route to take to approach your targeted pool of customers and reach them in a way that will prompt them to respond positively.

The joy of living in our digital age is that we have a vast array of communication channels open to us, from video and social media to print media and directly communicated messages. When you know where your target audience "hangs out" on the Internet and in real life, you can reach them more effectively with messages designed to attract their attention.

How do you build a strategic communications plan?

The foundation of it all is the key message you want to tell people about your company. This is the message that will be included in every single exchange of information about your company. It needs to be simple and memorable and send exactly the tone and value by which you want to be known.

Determining what that message is precisely is difficult, but once you have it, everything else falls into place.

To determine that message, you need to understand exactly what your perspective is on your business (or the perspective of your partners or board members if you have them) and couple that with an intense understanding of each customer's unique resistance to that message, their goals, desires and fears. If you have a wide range of different kinds of clients, you will need to draw up observations and sub-observations so that each category is covered. Ultimately, you may end up having a main message and a series of sub-messages geared to unique client bases.

If you don't have the one over-riding message, be aware that people's trust in you and your company is diminished each time they hear a different version of your message. They start to wonder what you really stand for.

A comprehensive message should let all people know the vision of your company, its objectives, its achievements, its products and services offered and how it delivers accountability to the public and specifically to its customers.

Involve your team in building your key message. Get them started by re-connecting them to the company's mission statement and vision. Talk to them about how the company has to change and grow to keep its customer base happy and attract new customers. What is the big idea that your company needs to have that keeps your customers intrigued?

I will share with you my own process for developing my key messages so that you can see how it leads you closer.

For example, when I started to think about my big idea, the glue that binds all my efforts together, I wrote:

"I want to be remembered as the instigator of the right to dream again and encourage people to live boldly. As we emerge into a new industrial revolution, the challenges before us will be unlike any civilization has faced in history. We need to unleash our imaginations and our confidence and envision new ways that we can work with each other and with machines to create value. We need to be skilled in the art of re-invention and bold in taking steps where we haven't gone before."

Many companies use finding their key message as a process of re-branding as they prepare their strategic communications plan.

Whatever message ideas are put forward, they have to be weighed and measured on their possible impact on your targeted customers. Keep in mind that the key message of your company will be aimed primarily at your customers, but it will also impact your employees, your investors, your board, and your community.

Think about the action that you hope people will take as a result of hearing your message. Are you trying to build up yourself as an authority in your field? Are you trying to push people into a sales funnel? Are you trying to create awareness about what you do and why it is important? Are you focused on a cause that is greater than your company?

Again, going back to my own exercise, I considered

how my vision could contribute to a new "return on investment" for the world. I wrote:

"My vision enlivens and empowers people and helps them be the best in the purposeful work that they do. I push them to dream big and to take bold action for the betterment of themselves and their companies. How does this impact the bottom line? It improves productivity and sales but, more importantly, it creates value in the person and in the world. We need to stay focused on ROI, of course, but we cannot let that be a blinder shutting off all the other ways our companies need to evolve in the future."

Then you have to consider how you will communicate that message. Common venues are websites, presentations, printed marketing materials and news releases, blogs and articles on the Internet, and in traditional media.

Which of the many channels of communication will funnel your message most directly to your targeted audience? Is there a particular time of the year, or a season or even a time of the day when they will be most responsive to your message?

Identify all communication roads you are currently using to get your message out. Often what already exists remains a useful way to keep the lines of communication flowing.

You also have to consider your budget. If you cannot possibly allocate a significant amount of money to purchase advertising you have to find effective ways to get your message out more in other ways. Usually, that means word of mouth, social media, and emails. Larger budgets can include advertising campaigns in traditional and social media, direct mail campaigns, posters and other print material.

Remember, when planning how to reach your various customer groups that there is not just one road to each group. In fact, the more ways you can get a message to people, the more it starts to make an impression on them. It makes them think that talk of this is coming from many direction, and somehow that seems to make it more credible and more important.

Then you begin to build your communications roadmap. Make sure that every time you or your representative speaks for your company that the message is clear and consistent. Don't waste your resources and miss opportunities to bring customers on side by using a scatter-gun approach to your communications.

At this point, you have considered and defined your message, determined who should be receiving your message, and how you can reach them. You start to deliver that message and you may think that your strategic communications plan is complete.

It isn't. There are two more steps in the process.

First, you have to put in place strategies to measure responses to your message. Throughout this entire process, the most important thing is to consistently seek and consider feedback. Try to determine how your customers heard your message and were prompted to act on it. Which of the many avenues of communication you selected reached the greatest number of customers who ended up doing business with you?

Use surveys, follow-up calls and emails, and maintain a rigorous assessment process.

The final step of the strategic communication plan happens after everything has been put in place and the messages delivered for a specified period of time. Then you have to determine what worked best through your systems of measurement. Finally, you have to make adjustments to your plan to make it more effective.

You may discover that one sector of your customers respond very favorably to your message, but another sector finds it confusing or misunderstands it. You need to make corrections and adjustments.

How often should you review your plan?

At least once every quarter for minor tweaks, and a complete analysis should be done once a year. This is a change from earlier best practices that originally suggested every two years. But, the pace of communications and the tools used to accomplish it are changing so rapidly that two years is a lifetime in our digital world.

Why do you have to review it so frequently?

It is because when you made the plan you based it on the knowledge you and your team had of your company, your products and services, your customers, and the venues to reach them and the assumptions you made based on that knowledge.

But in a few short months, you may have seen the need for a new service or product and added it to your business mix and it may have taken off. Not only that, but its customers may have come from an entirely different sector than the ones you had targeted at the time of your plan. You have to be able to adjust quickly if you are going to take advantage of this new momentum.

Remember, that one single isolated event or circumstance can impact the world in an instant and change perceptions about something forever. Bombs released outside a mega-concert that injure and kill audience members change how parents feel about their children going to such events, for example.

What kind of new inventions are entering the marketplace that could change your customer's need for the product or service you are selling? Is what you do about to be automated? Is there still a clientele who will prefer the human touch? Can you incorporate the new technology into your business and benefit from it and pass on my value to your customers?

Once you bring your plan back in line with what is happening and how you are responding to it, it will stay relevant. You may also need to be heard on new social media sites or find yourself joining a networking initiative that allows you to bring your key message to a broader audience.

THE CONQUER ZONE

Take some time today to consider three key messages you want to send about yourself and your company to the world.

What is it that people need to know about what you do to convince them to trust you to provide your service or product to them?

Once you have honed your messages, use them over and over again, from casual conversations to your website to your printed material or public presentations.

ENERGIZER

"The art of communication is the language of leadership."

– James Humes

CHAPTER 12

HOW TO SAFEGUARD YOUR GROWING SUCCESS

"Part of courage is simple consistency."

– Peggy Noonan

N O MATTER WHAT kind of business you are in, no matter what kind of great service or innovative product you offer, the most important element that will guarantee your business success is consistency.

But it is not enough to be consistent if your consistency isn't moving your business forward. You need to be constantly aligning what you are doing with your business goals.

With consistency and alignment comes one other key element of a business success strategy my team and I have developed, and that is repetition.

When you produce the best product or service and it is aligned with your business goals, you have to find the resources to repeat your processes over and over again for success.

When you accomplish that, you have a smoothly operating business that is hitting its targets. That leaves you time as the visionary to think innovatively and develop new products and services and goals for the future.

In this final chapter, we are going to look at how you can keep your business on the growth track using our CAR Strategy (Consistency, Alignment and Repetition).

Consistency means conformity in the application of something. It means logical, orderly processes that follow the same pattern. It means your work is always up to par. It means people can depend on you.

You develop consistency in your business through good processes.

While most of us know that, we still have a tendency to operate by the skin of our teeth, completing work on a case-by-case basis, re-inventing a bit of the wheel each time we tackle a new gig.

It is a reality of small business that we never have enough time, people or money to make us feel like we are really riding the wave instead of chasing it.

But we can get in front if we set up a consistent process that guarantees standards and practices that are implemented with everything we do.

As a small business owner, you need to offer consistency in what you sell, whether it is a product or service. When you have standard processes in place you do not get sloppy in delivering quality, service, packaging or processes.

Let's say that you are a motivational speaker. Your client contacts you and asks about whether you can be keynote speaker at a corporate convention on the subject of inspiration.

Your first response can't be to immediately start writing an amazing presentation on that topic.

Your first step is to be consistent in your process. You should have a form that covers essential questions about your audience, the location for the address, the remuneration, the travel arrangements, and all the little details that allow both you and the person hiring you to know where you stand.

Your contract needs to be consistent, so that when a happy client recommends you to another and tells them how they arranged working with you the new referral gets basically the same process.

Once those things are done, you create a consistently good presentation, speaking to the allotted time on the allotted subject.

You show up early, do all your consistent checks so there are no surprises awaiting you when you step up to speak, and then you deliver your consistently good presentation.

The event host knows you can be depended upon to stay and mingle briefly afterwards to talk with guests and to fulfill any other agreed-upon appearances or details.

In addition to being consistent with those who hire you, you have to be consistent with your customers.

Using the same example, if you normally speak in a humorous, casual style, you should be consistent in that approach. That way, if someone in the audience bought a ticket to hear you because they saw you before and loved your style, you are giving a consistent performance.

Please make sure that you know what your customers expect every time they do business with you and that you meet those expectations each and every time you do business together.

As long as you are consistent in your approach you will be able to do that.

If you are wildly inconsistent you will alienate your customers and fans and they will stop referring you to their friends and colleagues.

Consistency spreads further in your business, to your suppliers and operations management, for example.

Suppliers want to be paid consistently, which in business terms means always on time, every time. As a small business, it can sometimes be difficult to ensure that every account is settled on time. If you pay every month, but are always two days later because that is when a certain check comes into you, most will go along with that.

But if you are all over the calendar with your payment, you will inevitably run into problems with having your supplies when you need them.

The same thing goes with standardizing your business operations, whether you are providing a service, manufacturing or retailing. You do not want to be drowning in forms and red tape, but to have simple processes that are followed consistently to take and send orders or to contract your services, you will run a more professional operation than if you have to make it up each time.

Whenever we talk about consistency there are always people who feel rebellious about the concept. They are afraid that by being consistent they will become robotic or predictable or even boring. They equate consistency with stagnation.

It is not the same thing at all. Consistency is in fact a vehicle for safeguarding your growth. When you deliver your services or product to the same quality standard each time, they are more willing to sign long-term contracts with you, a key factor in maintaining consistent growth.

There is an old business adage reminding entrepreneurs not to put all their eggs in one basket. But once you start a business, you discover that your core business actually sits in one basket because it best reflects your skills and business opportunities.

Think of consistency as that package that protects your eggs. With eggs you can boil, fry, bake or poach them, turn them into quiches, dye them as decorations and do many of the things that your creative mind comes up with.

But you cannot do any of those creative things if your eggs don't arrive safely in a good package. You expect to bring them home and find them usable, not a gooey mass of yolk and whites rolling along in a shopping bag. Consistency is the package of your business; you can do what you want with the key ingredients once you get them to their destination safely.

Consistency in business is something you can measure to determine if it is working or not. Is the process saving you time or money? Is it making your products or services better? Is it streamlining everyday matters of business? That is how you measure consistency.

It also creates accountability from you and your staff.

Going back to our CAR triangle, the next factor is alignment, and by that, I mean the strategic alignment.

For your company to stay on the right track as it

grows you need to ensure that your strategic goals, your business processes and models, and your corporate culture are all aligned to the key purpose and core values on which your business is based.

Just as your vehicle drives better, straighter and more efficiently when your wheels are aligned, so too does your company move forward more effectively when your methods and goals are aligned.

In fact, failure to align your company strategically is another major cause of business failure.

If your company members can't quickly and forthrightly answer the question "Why are we in business?", then your business is out of alignment and needs an immediate adjustment.

Losing sight of your purpose is the beginning of the end for most businesses. Yet it can happen when you get on the fast track of business growth. Growth and diversification, as great as they are as forces to move your company forward, can also cause you to lose sight of your center.

If what your business really stands for has become a blur you need to stop and recalculate the future of your organization. If your processes and culture aren't united, or if you see signs that your business has become self-centered instead of customer centered, then you have a huge problem.

Issues with alignment are more common than you might think.

According to Entrepreneurs' magazine, sixty-five percent of organizations have an agreed-upon strategy, but only fourteen percent of their employees understand what that strategy is. Can you see how easily misalignment can happen?

If your company has fallen out of alignment, how do you work your way back?

When most companies realize they are out of alignment they are tempted to make a knee-jerk response to go in one of two directions.

In the first instance, they decide that their internal mission is valid and regardless of the issues they are facing, they will stick with it. They make comments like "We are who we are and if customers don't like it, too bad!"

In the second instance, you realize you are out of alignment with your customers and you respond by starting to accommodate their every whim.

That doesn't work either, of course, because you cannot possibly please everyone.

Both approach one and approach two, although on opposite sides of the alignment process, will be unsustainable.

What you really need to do to align your company is to ask yourself every few months these two questions:

1. What will my customers buy?

2. What am I producing or selling?

If the answers to these two questions aren't aligned it is a clear signal that your tires are flat and you will soon be running off the road.

You have to be moving forward in the direction of your customers' needs. Your staff also need to be aware of this, so that all efforts are moving forward in a direct path, not from side to side at the whim of different agendas.

When you need to realign go back to your initial goals and objectives in starting your business and then measure your strategies against them. If your strategies are not advancing your goals, you are stumbling. Your strategies are the means by which you implement your goals.

If you have many different goals, you will need many different strategies, but they will all have to be working in unison to achieve those goals. The strategies must work together, not against each other.

It is your job as the CEO to ensure that you are constantly looking at the big picture to make sure that your strategies are not hindering your progress.

Even your operations need to be aligned to your strategies. The operation of your company refers to the actual work that is done, the daily tasks that are completed. They are the means by which your goals and strategies become action, one step at a time.

When you own a small business you have limited staff and resources, that is the nature of the beast. So your operational strategies have to be carefully aligned to ensure that the efforts being made are moving you in the direction you need to go.

The final component of the "CAR" triangle of good business practices is repetition.

Because most people who start their own businesses are quick-thinkers they have a tendency to undervalue repetition and consider it a real annoyance. They see it is a detriment, a time-waster. Isn't saying and doing something once enough? Isn't demonstrating a new skill to your staff once quite enough?

It turns out that with your staff and your customers, sharing vital information is never sufficient if it is done just once.

People have a lot on their minds these days and so many urgent things competing for their attention. Remembering your values, your product, your service and you isn't top of their list.

It is always a mistake to assume that because you told

a customer something once that they will remember it each time. They won't.

You need to find new and effective ways to repeat your messages and offerings over and over again.

You need to tell your staff about the processes you want filed again and again until it is their second nature.

You need to tell your sales team about your products and services so often that they remember it unconsciously and in different contexts when they are meeting with clients

And you need to tell your clients about your business in a variety of different avenues, from verbally to written to audio to visual and all combinations in between. You have to assume that sometimes they are not listening at all, sometimes they are half-listening, and rarely are they truly listening.

Repeat, repeat, repeat.

What does this mean for you as the business owner or leader? Do you have to repeat things for yourself as well as for everyone else?

It turns out that you do.

Remember that each time you do something it falls into one of two categories. It is something that you have done before, or something that you are doing for the first time.

If you have done something before, there are still more categories. Is it something that you have done often before, or something that you have done rarely before?

If you haven't done it before, there are also more categories. Is the task something that you will do once and likely never do it again, or will it be an action that once learned will be repeated?

A big part of being effective with your time, knowledge and energy is managing these different types of actions and deciding which ones you should perform only once, which ones you should do many times, and which ones you should not be doing at all.

Repetition of tasks is vital to keeping your business on track. It is the cornerstone of all business dating as far back as when Adam Smith defined which tasks we do repetitively and which ones we do rarely. He called it the "division of labor."

If you need to do a task repetitively, you need to find processes that make it as simple as possible and accomplished it as quickly as possible. You may also need to find a way to train another person to do this task, since it is so repetitive.

The whole idea when you repeat tasks is to break them down into smaller tasks and smaller tasks than that so that you have a process that is easy to follow and repeat.

If you use Six Sigma or TQM in your business, you will know that the goal of breaking all big tasks down into small ones is the ultimate goal for smooth processes.

As business owners, you will use repetition in your own work to build administrative systems that are streamlined and workable. You will use repetition as a tool to predict and plan the future by noting which events and cycles repeat themselves predictably. You will be able to use repetition of use of supplies to purchase certain things in bulk knowing you will need frequent repeat orders.

When you see tasks that need to be endlessly repeated, you can study technology to see if you can automate that service.

You can also use repetition as a training tool to help your team become highly familiar with your business goals and processes.

In Japan, the concept of repetition in business is highly praised so that every nuance of every task is studied with an eye to determining if it can be modified to be done faster or better. They build whole business discussions around what they refer to as repetition with modification.

Sometimes in business you need to have unique actions because you are launching a new series, innovating a new product or moving in a new direction.

But many times, you just have to have the same single action repeated again and again.

If you struggle with the concept of repetition, remember that as human beings, repetitive actions are a key to our survival and sustainability. We sleep and we awake every 24 hours. We eat at least three times a day normally. We exercise normally doing repetitive cycles of action.

In the morning when you get up, you likely repeat your actions from the day before, perhaps having a coffee and your usual preferred breakfast. At the end of the day, you may watch your favorite television shows, week after week. We drive or commute the same way to work each day or start work around the same time each day in our home office.

It is the repetition of these comfortable routines that help us manage the unpredictable things that happen in our lives. They reassure us that we are okay and give us a high level of comfort.

Repetition in our lives helps us do more and be more efficient, for the most part. We don't have to rethink our simple tasks and routines every single day. We do things almost automatically.

In the workplace, it is a way of increasing our productivity and gives us a framework for management. It helps us train others and look after basics of business that are vital to our sustainability.

Repetition is a human impulse and managing it is a key aspect of running your business successfully.

Having said that, remember that no repetitive action goes on forever. Ultimately, the cycle of repetition always ends. Your customers change, your markets evolve, your staff moves on and you find new apps and methods to do tasks. You drop old products when the response lowers, you pivot with new offerings and strategies.

Repetition changes also because every time you do a task, even the same task, you may feel differently or approach it from a different angle. As Heraclitus, the Greek philosopher noted, "No man can step into the same river twice." The man is different and the river is different, because being alive changes us every day.

But having said that, we can still break down our tasks between those we do rarely and those we do constantly and refine our abilities to do both.

THE CONQUER ZONE

First, in your efforts to be consistent in your company, what is your process for completing the onboarding of a new client at the point that they agree to purchase your service or product? Do you use a standardized contract? What are the key components of that contract? Do you send an email defining the agreement? Take a few minutes and write out that process.

Next, consider what your customers buy from you. What products or services do you sell? Are what they buy and what you sell in alignment?

Finally, make a list of all tasks that you must repeat week after week. Can they be out-sourced? Is there a way to simplify them further? Consider your options.

ENERGIZER

"Every successful organization has to make the transition from a world defined primarily by repetition to one primarily defined by change. This is the biggest transformation in the structure of how humans work together since the Agricultural Revolution."

– Bill Drayton

CONCLUSION

WHETHER YOU ABSORB this book a chapter at a time or as a full and lengthy read, I hope that it has helped you to see that growing your business is possible if you take a holistic approach and bring each part of it gently forward in our evolving world of work.

Behind each chapter is the underlying message that you will see change in your business world when you see change within yourself.

Your self-enlightenment, as you learn about the different ways your business can grow, will re-energize your business and your personal world as well. You will begin to use your time wisely, to consider solid strategies and set a workable plan for growth.

You will begin to incorporate the Consistency, Alignment and Repetition (CAR) strategy in every project you tackle.

My goal in creating this book is that you will not just grow your business as a corporate survival mechanism, but as a way to recognize the value of yourself and the work that you do. In that process, you will also come to better recognize the value of others, your customers and colleagues, and when that happens, your world will change in a magnificent way.

ABOUT THE AUTHOR

PAULA MORAND is a leadership building, revenue boosting, strategy expanding, keynote speaker, author and visionary. This dreaming big and being bold leadership expert and brand strategist brings her vibrant energy, humour and wisdom to ignite individuals, organizations and communities to lead change, growth and impact in a more bold fashion. 24 years, 27,000 clients, 34 countries, 15 books, former radio personality, 11x award winning entrepreneur and humorous emcee. Check out Paula's best selling books: *"Bold Courage: How Owning Your Awesome Changes Everything"*, *"Dreaming BIG and Being BOLD: Inspiring stories from Trailblazers, Visionaries and Change Makers"* book. Find out more by visiting www. paulamorand.com

BIBLIOGRAPHY

Morand, Paul. Bold Courage: How Owning Your Awesome Changes Everything. 2016. Motivational Press https://www.amazon.com/Bold-Courage-Awesome-Changes-Everything-ebook/dp/B01M7URG-JW

Fisk, Peter. The Innovation Mindset. Article. 2015. Published on The Genius Works Website. http://www.thegeniusworks.com/event/the-innovation-mindset/

Govindarajan, Vijay and Srinivas, Srikanth. The Innovation Mindset in Action: 3M Corporation. Article published on line August 6, 2013. Harvard Business Review https://hbr.org/2013/08/the-innovation-mindset-in-acti-3

Sugars, Brad. 5 Ways to Grow Your Profits: A simple formula to maximize profit margins. Article published on line Aug. 14, 2009 on Entrepreneur https://www.entrepreneur.com/article/203046

Gingiss, Dan. How Social Media Has Changed the Game for Customer Services. Dec. 13, 2016. Social Media Today website http://www.socialmediatoday.com/special-columns/how-social-media-has-changed-game-customer-service

American Express: Customers Reward Outstanding Service by Spending More and Spreading the Word to Friends and Family. News Release published on website Oct. 28, 2014 http://about.americanexpress.com/news/pr/2014/outstanding-service-spend-more-spread-word.aspx

Watermark Consulting – The 2015 Customer Experience ROI Study: Demonstrating the business value of a great customer experience. Published on their website: http://watermarkconsult.net/docs/Watermark-Customer-Experience-ROI-Study.pdf

Springer, Tom et all. What it takes to win with customer experience. July 8, 2011. Published on Bain & Company website http://www.bain.com/publications/articles/what-it-takes-to-win-with-customer-experience.aspx

Temkins Experience Ratings Report 2016. March 8, 2016. Released on Temkins website. https://experiencematters.blog/2016/03/08/report-2016-temkin-experience-ratings/

The Excellence Center Team. KPMG Nunwood. Customer Experience Strategy: How Zappos became a 2016 US top ten customer brand. May 25, 2016 https://experiencematters.blog/2016/03/08/report-2016-temkin-experience-ratings/

Zorfas, Alan and Leemon, Daniel. An Emotional Connection Matters More than Customer

Satisfaction. Aug. 29, 2016. Harvard Business Review https://hbr.org/2016/08/an-emotional-connection-matters-more-than-customer-satisfaction

Nutt, Paul C. Why Decisions Fail. July 15, 2002. Berrett-Koehler Publishers https://www.amazon.com/Why-Decisions-Fail-Paul-Nutt/dp/1576751503

Heath, Chip and Sivony, Olivier. Making great decisions. April 2013. Mckinsey Quarterly http://www.mckinsey.com/business-functions/strategy-and-corporate-finance/our-insights/making-great-decisions

Heath, Chip and Heath, Dan. Decisive: How to make better choices in life and work. March 26, 2013. Crown Business. https://www.amazon.com/Decisive-Make-Better-Choices-Life/dp/0307956393

Snowden, David J., Boone, Mary E. A Leader's Framework for Decision Making. November, 2007 Harvard Business Review. https://hbr.org/2007/11/a-leaders-framework-for-decision-making

CPSIA information can be obtained
at www.ICGtesting.com
Printed in the USA
LVOW13s0417280318
571384LV00001B/1/P